VASSA ZHELEZNOVA

A MOTHER

English translation by
TANIA ALEXANDER and TIM SUTER

AMBER LANE PRESS

First published in 1988 by
Amber Lane Press Ltd.
9 Middle Way
Oxford OX2 7LH

Typeset and printed in Great Britain by
Cotswold Press Ltd., Eynsham, Oxford

ISBN 0 906399 83 1

INTRODUCTION

Gorky wrote the first version of *Vassa Zheleznova* in 1909 while living in exile in Italy. There was a saying in Nizhni Novgorod, where Gorky was born in 1868 and which is now named after him: "The houses are made of stone — the people of iron." Gorky remembered this and in real life had come across such iron people. In particular he remembered several powerful and ruthless women who dominated the commercial life of Nizhni Novgorod, and who were to serve him as prototypes for his play *Vassa Zheleznova*. Nizhni Novgorod in Gorky's childhood was a small provincial town where the *meshchane*, the new petit bourgeois class, was beginning to make itself felt.

There are two versions of the play. Whereas the Vassa of the first version was to some extent based on a variety of real life characters, Vassa of the second version (written in 1935) is modelled to a much greater extent on one real life character, Maria Kapitonovna Kashina — ''the shrewd proprietress of a large shipping concern'', as Gorky described her in a letter to Olga Forsh in 1926.

The two versions differ widely in both tone and content. Gorky wrote the second version in December 1935 but died before he could see a stage performance. It was in fact during a rehearsal of a revival of the first version at the Moscow Arts Theatre in 1935 that he telegraphed to the producer, I.N. Berseyev: "Please stop all rehearsals. In January I shall submit a completely new text." But nobody expected the second version to differ so much from the first. It was in fact a completely new play. The only similarity between the two plays was in the title and in the names — and even there Vassa's patronymic has been changed from Petrovna to Borisovna. Even the location of the play changed from the small provincial Russian town of Gorky's childhood to a large city on the Volga. Vassa's husband is no longer the narrow-minded *meshchanin*, the representative of the petit bourgeoisie in Russia who has only recently shed his peasant roots and has managed to build up a brick and tile business. In the new version he becomes a member of the wealthy merchant class, the ruthless head of a vast shipping concern on the Volga, who has married the boss's daughter to enhance his career. Gorky also brought a new political element into the play by introducing an entirely new character, Rachel, a social revolutionary who challenges Vassa and all the values of the past.

Gorky insisted that the second version should be the definitive version and not an alternative play. It is this version that has been in the repertoire of the Moscow Arts Theatre and has also been turned into a great Soviet film. It is the play that most people know. However, from time to time the first version is still played on the Russian stage and as recently as 1979 Anatoly Vassilyev directed it in Moscow.

It is easy to see why Gorky felt that his play needed such drastic revision. From 1921 to 1933 he had again been living out of Russia, and the country he returned to was greatly changed. The *meshchanin* no longer existed, and the sharply political atmosphere of the thirties seemed to require a play where the clashes between the characters were more starkly drawn and politically motivated than had been called for in 1909 when the first version was written.

But whatever Gorky may have felt at the time, a great deal was lost in the 1935 version. The first play, published here for the first time in English, has a strength and unity of theme and structure, and a warmth in the characterisation that are lacking in the second version. It is first and foremost a remarkable study of the central character, Vassa Petrovna. At its core is the struggle for the inheritance of Zahar Zheleznov, who is on his death bed. Vassa's children and brother-in-law want to take their share out of the business and move away from the family. But Vassa, a passionate matriarch, is prepared to commit crime to preserve the business she and her husband have sweated to build up, and to keep the family together. To this end she arranges the forgery of her husband's will; is a party to the murder of her brother-in-law, the 'enemy of the family'; sends a son into a monastery and browbeats her other children. The Vassa of the first version does not set out to grab the business for herself. The motivation of her behaviour is the preservation of the family and the protection of the inheritance for her children and grandchildren. Gorky's subtitle for the play was 'A Mother'. "I too am a mother," Vassa says to her daughter Anna, "remember, for the sake of your children, in their interest, nothing is shameful, nothing is ever a sin." The play is a strong attack on the *meshchane* class, the beginnings of petit bourgeois values and materialistic attitudes which destroy the family. It is also about the corruption of human feelings and decency by material possessions. Gorky shows us how Vassa's human and maternal feelings are misguided. Due to the bourgeois values which she has acquired she is unable to see any other way by which the family can be kept together except by holding onto the business and the money.

Gorky was always fascinated — even in private life — by strong women. The study of the central character, torn by her internal struggle and the tragedy of finding herself fighting against her children while fighting for them, is so powerful that in spite of all the terrible things she does we can't help feeling some sympathy for her. The strength and ruthlessness of her character alternately arouse feelings of repulsion and sympathy in us.

* * *

This translation of *Vassa Zheleznova* was first performed as part of BBC Radio 3's major Russian Season on 11th November 1986. Clearly the play as broadcast differed in some respects from the version prepared here for the stage.

Radio as a dramatic medium requires more movement and variation than a stage play. The radio version of *Vassa Zheleznova* treated the play filmically, moving at will around Vassa's house and its grounds. Discussions about the business and plotting with Mihail took place in Vassa's small cramped office; big family scenes were set in larger spaces. The murder of Prokhor itself took place in Prokhor's bedroom, the play briefly following the action there; while Liudmila's great set piece at the start of Act Two, where she speaks so lovingly and longingly of Vassa's garden, was set in the garden itself, the only time the sounds of nature were allowed to intrude into the darkening world of the play.

For the most part these changes required very little modification of Gorky's text, for the action moves within clearly defined sections. Only the third act was slightly re-structured to make the narrative line easier for the radio audience, and to clarify motivations that on stage are largely unspoken; but throughout, the broadcast version remained faithful to Gorky's narrative and his intentions.

For this publication we have restored the original shape and structure of Gorky's powerful study.

T.A. & T.S.

CHARACTERS

VASSA PETROVNA ZHELEZNOVA
ANNA ⎫
SEMYON ⎬ her children
PAVEL ⎭
NATALYA — Semyon's wife
LIUDMILA — Pavel's wife and Mihail's daughter
PROKHOR ZHELEZNOV — Zahar's brother and Vassa's
    brother-in-law
MIHAIL VASSILYEV — the manager
DUNYA — a distant relative of the Zheleznovs
LIPA — the maid

ZAHAR ZHELEZNOV — Vassa's husband — does not appear

The play takes place in 1909 in a small provincial town on the Volga.

A radio version of this play, *Vassa Zheleznova*, was broadcast by BBC Radio 3, as part of the Russian Season, on 11th November 1986. The cast was as follows:

VASSA	Billie Whitelaw
PROKHOR:	Robert Lang
ANNA:	Emily Richard
LIUDMILA:.	Wendy Morgan
SEMYON:	Andrew Branch
PAVEL:	Jonathan Tafler
MIHAIL:	Denis Lill
NATALYA:	Sue Broomfield
LIPA:	Elaine Claxton
DUNYA:	Sheila Grant

Producer: Matthew Walters

Billie Whitelaw was awarded the Sony Radio Award for the Best Actress, 1986, for her performance in this production.

ACT ONE

Early winter morning. A large room, which is VASSA ZHELEZNOVA's bedroom and her office. The room seems cluttered up. In one corner behind a screen is a bed; to the left of it a table covered with papers held down by tiles, which serve as paperweights. Next to the table is a tall desk and in front of the window a sofa. Several lamps with green shades. In the right corner is a tiled stove with a flat top and next to it a safe and a door leading to a chapel. Various papers are pinned to the screen and as you pass them they rustle. Upstage there are wide doors leading into the dining room; one can see the table with a chandelier hanging above it. On the table is a lighted candle.

DUNYA is laying the tea in the dining room. LIPA brings in a steaming samovar.

DUNYA: Is she back yet?

LIPA: No.

DUNYA: Oh dear, what's going to happen?

LIPA: I really don't know.

> [*She enters VASSA's room and looks around. VASSA enters from the door leading to the chapel.*]

VASSA: You're late, Lipa! What time do you call this? It's quarter past seven!

LIPA: I'm sorry, Vassa Petrovna, but Zahar Ivanovich was taken bad again, early this morning.

VASSA: Hm. No telegram from Anna yet?

LIPA: No.

VASSA: Where's everyone else? Are they up yet?

LIPA: Well, Pavel Zaharovich didn't go to bed at all —

VASSA: Don't say he's ill as well!

LIPA: No, madam, he was waiting up for his wife. But Liudmila Mihailovna wasn't here last night. I don't know where she can have been or who she was with . . .

VASSA: Watch it, Lipa, I'm warning you . . .

LIPA: Me? Why?

VASSA: You like the taste of bad news, don't you? It gives you a thrill, eh?

LIPA: Vassa Petrovna, I only —

VASSA: Oh shut up and get out.

LIPA: Yes, madam.

VASSA: Go and tell everyone tea's ready in the dining room. Dunya, bring mine in here. And Lipa —

LIPA: Yes?

VASSA: Listen: don't wake Liudmila if she's still sleeping. She spent last night with her father. Is that clear?

LIPA: Yes, Vassa Petrovna.

VASSA: Has Mihail Vassilyevich arrived yet?

LIPA: Yes, madam.

VASSA: Good. Tell him I want to see him. Now.

LIPA: Yes, madam.

> [*LIPA exits. DUNYA enters with VASSA's tea.*]

DUNYA: Good morning, Vassa dear.

VASSA: Yes, good morning. Well, what are you looking so worried about?

DUNYA: It's Zahar Ivanovich; he's been so unwell in the night, madam.

VASSA: [*sharp*] Did he say anything?

DUNYA: Oh no. Well, he couldn't. He could scarcely even move his eyelids.

VASSA: Listen, Dunya, they'll all be coming to tea soon. I want you to listen carefully to what they say about Liudmila, and then tell me. All right?

DUNYA: Yes, of course, Vassa. And pray God all will be well.

VASSA: Yes, yes. That's enough now. Give me my tea and go. Remember what I said.

DUNYA: Of course.

> [*She goes. VASSA puts her hands on the writing desk, frowns and pushes her spectacles up onto her forehead, muttering under her breath. MIHAIL enters.*]

MIHAIL: You wanted to see me.

VASSA: Where has your daughter got to, then? Call yourself a parent!

MIHAIL: Vassa, for God's sake, there is nothing I can do, nothing at all. It's all beyond me.

VASSA: She's made my son a laughing stock!

MIHAIL: And what has he done to her, then?

VASSA: Listen. If anybody asks, she spent last night with you. Got that?

MIHAIL: Yes, all right.

VASSA: The stupid little girl needs her arse tanned. [*laughs*] Wouldn't do any good, I suppose.

MIHAIL: No, I don't suppose it would. But be careful how much you blame her. Don't forget: she never wanted to get married in the first place. You knew that, and you knew it hadn't a chance of working, but you forced them into it.

VASSA: Oh yes? And you, I suppose, are quite blameless? [*Pause.*] You've been with Zahar? How is he?

MIHAIL: He's . . . ill.

VASSA: But has he signed yet?

MIHAIL: No, not yet. I'll have to —

VASSA: What about the priest? Did he agree?

MIHAIL: Yes, for five hundred roubles. The greedy . . .

VASSA: Who cares? Why shouldn't he make a bit out of it? And the others? Ryzhev and Muhoyedov?

MIHAIL: All taken care of.

VASSA: Good. We must have a careful think after all this is over; we've still got the children to deal with.

MIHAIL: Yes, I know; they could make trouble for us if they wanted to . . .

VASSA: Why hasn't Anna come, that's what I want to know. No word from her, nothing.

> [*Noise off in the dining room.*]

Shush, there's someone . . . Dunya, is that you? [*Silence.*] Who's there?

PAVEL: [*in the dining room*] It's me, Pavel.

VASSA: What in God's name are you hiding for? Are you afraid of me? Come in and say good morning to your mother at least.

> [*PAVEL enters.*]

PAVEL: Very well then, good morning, Mother. And you here, my respected father-in-law? Where's your daughter, then? Eh?

MIHAIL: Don't ask me. [*going*] The church and the law handed her over to you — I thought you were meant to look after her.

> [*MIHAIL exits.*]

PAVEL: Oh God, I feel so . . . so humiliated. My own wife. Mother, please help me; what am I going to do?

VASSA: All right, that's enough, be patient.

PAVEL: Patient? Don't you hear what I'm saying? I can't take it any more.

VASSA: I told you, right at the start, she's not right for you! Why
    didn't you listen to me? Why couldn't you have married some-
    one . . . oh, I don't know, someone quiet and gentle.

PAVEL: Why don't you say what you mean, Mother? A cripple, you
    mean. A freak like me. That's what you think, isn't it? I should
    have married someone crippled and twisted like myself? Well
    go on, say it!

VASSA: Stop it! [*blows out the candles*] All this complaining — you
    only make yourself even more of a laughing stock than you al-
    ready are. Now shut up!

PAVEL: Aren't you ashamed too, Mother? My wife is a whore. Dear
    God, Pavel Zaharovich Zheleznov's wife a whore!

VASSA: I said shut up! Pull yourself together — go and get your-
    self some tea or something. [*aside*] Why does God choose me
    to be blessed with you? He really ought to keep such holy fools
    to Himself.

PAVEL: It's this place, I must get out, get away, go into town. How
    can I, though? I've got no money, you've got it all.

VASSA: How heartless can you get? Your father lies dying, and you
    want to go off into the town —

PAVEL: [*throwing himself onto the sofa*] What else can I do?
        [*NATALYA enters from the dining room.*]

NATALYA: Oh, I'm so sorry . . .

VASSA: Ah, Natalya, where have you been? It's late for you to be
    down.

NATALYA: I'm sorry, Vassa Petrovna; the fact is I was with Zahar
    Ivanovich until 3 o'clock this morning . . . What's wrong, Pavel?

VASSA: Oh, ignore him — he's just whining again. Pull yourself
    together. Dear God, I should have had you put down when
    you were born.

PAVEL: Yes, I know, Mother. You don't give a damn about my
    shame, you're just ashamed of me. Well, what are you staring
    at, Natalya? Oh leave me alone, all of you, I don't need any-
    thing.

NATALYA: Pavel, please don't get so worked up —

PAVEL: Don't touch me! Get away from me. I don't want your
    charity. I disgust you, don't I? I'm a freak, a cripple, my wife's
    a whore — just leave me alone!
        [*PAVEL exits.*]

NATALYA: [*following*] Oh Pavel, please let me . . .

[*NATALYA exits. MIHAIL enters.*]

MIHAIL: Vassa, I must talk with you urgently.

VASSA: Well, what now?

MIHAIL: I don't know how to say this. It's Liudmila — and her uncle . . .

VASSA: Prokhor! Where are they?

MIHAIL: At the farm. That's who she's been with all night.

VASSA: Oh thank God. For a terrible moment I thought you meant they'd gone for good. And Pavel? Does he know?

MIHAIL: He'll find out. He's bound to. [*Pause.*] I'm frightened . . . My daughter's ruined, and on top of that, the business that we've spent all our lives building up, it's falling apart . . .

VASSA: Stop moaning about it! You don't find me sitting and moaning. What good would it do?

MIHAIL: I haven't a hope while that man —

VASSA: You mean Prokhor?

MIHAIL: Can't you see — that man is danger, to all of us!

VASSA: I said, stop complaining. We'll soon see about the business falling apart . . .

MIHAIL: [*passionately*] Everybody thinks he's so conscience-stricken . . . Damn it, I know about that sort of rubbish, conscience and kindness. I can see through that lot. In real business they're about as much use as sand in a machine. It's all one big game. Who wants kindness? Nobody. No, give me what I'm worth, that's all I want; you can keep all that kindness rubbish for yourself. And as for conscience, people only play that one to get attention; and then what happens? Everybody cries buckets and feels good, but nobody actually does any work. I tell you, that man is danger.

VASSA: All right; and what are you going to do about him?

MIHAIL: Me? [*Pause.*] Well . . .

VASSA: Well go on, I'm waiting.

MIHAIL: [*after a moment*] . . . I'll choose my moment. Anyway, oughtn't you to be going to see your husband?

VASSA: Yes, I suppose I ought to. [*Pause.*] And still no word from Anna, not a single word.

[*She is making for the door.*]

MIHAIL: I can't understand why you set such hopes on her; I don't see what she —

VASSA: [*turning to face him*] You know nothing about her — so shut
up!

MIHAIL: Oh God, life's so difficult . . .
[*He follows her.*]

VASSA: Maybe, but an easy life . . . well, they tell me the brain goes
sooner if you have an easy life.
[*They exit together. DUNYA enters from the dining room
and sits down, crossing herself.*]

DUNYA: Lord preserve and have mercy upon your servants wherever they may be, oh Lord.
[*LIPA enters.*]

LIPA: Where's the mistress? She's back!

DUNYA: Who? Anna?

LIPA: No, no: Liudmila! She only spent the night with her uncle!
Honestly, the things that go on here —
[*SEMYON enters.*]

SEMYON: Such as?

LIPA: Oh, sir, I didn't know . . . Nothing, sir, nothing at all.
[*LIPA exits.*]

SEMYON: Nothing, eh? Idiot. Dunya, good morning. Get me a
cup of tea, will you?

DUNYA: Of course, Semyon dear.
[*She goes into the dining room.*]

SEMYON: How's my father getting on?

DUNYA: [*from the dining room*] Oh dear, I'm afraid he's not at all
well.

SEMYON: Yes, well, he's been "not at all well" for months, hasn't
he? Where's everybody else? Have they all eaten?

DUNYA: [*entering*] Poor Pavel couldn't eat a thing this morning.

SEMYON: Oh? Why not?

DUNYA: Well, Liudmila . . . I don't know how to say this. His wife
didn't spend the night here last night.

SEMYON: You mean . . .

DUNYA: Yes, yes; and with Prokhor, apparently. Her husband's
uncle, no less. What Zahar would say —

SEMYON: Well, good lord. So he made it, did he? Well done,
Uncle Prokhor!

DUNYA: Made it? Yes, well . . . But the shame of it, Semyon, just
think of the shame!

SEMYON: It'll wipe the sickly grin off Pavel's face, that's for sure!

[*PROKHOR enters.*]

PROKHOR: I'll kill him, I swear to God I'll kill him . . . Where is he?

SEMYON: Speak of the devil. Who do you mean, Uncle Prokhor?

PROKHOR: That idiot cripple nephew of mine. Do you know what he's done? Only let the bloody cat in amongst my pigeons again. I'm so angry I could . . . oh, I don't know.

SEMYON: Anyway, Uncle, why do you look so bleary and dishevelled? Anyone would think you'd been sleeping . . . well, shall we say rough? Wouldn't they, Dunya?

PROKHOR: Would they? Yes, maybe I do look a bit of a mess. I suppose I'd better go and change.

SEMYON: Yes, you should.

PROKHOR: Dunya, make yourself useful and bring me some tea.

DUNYA: Yes, of course.

[*DUNYA exits.*]

PROKHOR: That damn Pavel's a menace. Do you know that cat got three pigeons — one white, two mottled.

SEMYON: But Uncle, what on earth could Pavel possibly have against you?

PROKHOR: Just watch it, Semyon. Don't push your luck. He's an idiot. He's certainly no match for that wife of his. My God, what a woman. She should go on the stage or something . . . So much passion.

[*LIPA enters.*]

LIPA: Excuse me, Prokhor Ivanovich —

PROKHOR: Well, what is it?

LIPA: The manager, Mihail Vassilyev, would like to see you.

PROKHOR: Oh, would he? Well, I'm the only manager as far as you're concerned, girl. I won't talk to him. And anyway, you're just snooping around again, aren't you? Listening in. Your ears are always flapping. Well, you can get out.

LIPA: But sir, what should I say to Mihail Vassilyev?

PROKHOR: Anything. Tell him I'm invisible. Tell Mihail he's an idiot and a swindler. Just get out, all right?

[*LIPA exits.*]

SEMYON: I know you don't like Mihail, but even so, how can an idiot possibly be a swindler?

PROKHOR: In this business, I tell you, even the swindlers are stupid, and Mihail is the stupidest of the lot.

SEMYON: Oh Uncle Prokhor, I do love to see you angry. You're so funny when you get angry.

PROKHOR: Oh very witty, Semyon, very witty indeed.

> [*LIUDMILA enters in her dressing gown. PROKHOR, embarrassed, clears his throat. LIUDMILA takes the tea DUNYA has just brought in for PROKHOR.*]

LIUDMILA: A little more milk for me, please Dunya.

> [*DUNYA, looking disapproving, coughs quietly and goes out again.*]

And what are you so happy about, eh, Semyon?

SEMYON: Liudmila, my dear Liudmila, the sight of you alone is enough to make all creation rejoice.

PROKHOR: Yes, even an animal like you.

SEMYON: Oh very good, Uncle Prokhor; very droll.

> [*DUNYA enters with the milk.*]

LIUDMILA: Can you believe it, Dunya? His father is lying there dying, and all he can do is sit and snigger. I wish you'd taught him to behave, like you taught me.

SEMYON: Listen, Liudmila, what am I supposed to do? Father's been at death's door for more than six months now —

PROKHOR: Always a decisive man, but now he can't make up his mind to die.

DUNYA: Oh . . . oh God . . .

PROKHOR: What is it now? Did I say something?

LIUDMILA: Hush, Dunya, just go and get on with your work. Uncle Prokhor has absolutely no morals. You shouldn't be in the room with him in the first place. Now go on.

DUNYA: Yes, Liudmila.

> [*She exits.*]

LIUDMILA: I don't like spies. Now listen, Prokhor, my Spaniard—

SEMYON: Yes, he looks like one.

PROKHOR: And when have you ever seen a Spaniard?

SEMYON: I saw one once, performing in a circus. Very appropriate.

LIUDMILA: Listen, Prokhor, I just came in to say that I'm going off now to catch up on some sleep, all right? But be ready about four; I'll be up around then.

SEMYON: You going for a ride?

LIUDMILA: Yes, in a troika.

PROKHOR: Why don't you come too? Bring that wife of yours along with you and we'll make a party of it.

SEMYON: Natalya? No, she'd never come. And then there's Pavel to think about . . .

LIUDMILA: What about him?

SEMYON: Well, it's . . . it's awkward, isn't it?

LIUDMILA: What's awkward about it?

SEMYON: I . . . well, I thought . . .
> [*He grins, embarrassed. PROKHOR looks at him, shaking his head sadly. VASSA enters.*]

VASSA: Semyon.

SEMYON: Ah, Mother; what is it?

VASSA: Leave us alone for a moment, will you?

SEMYON: But —

VASSA: Just go.
> [*SEMYON shrugs and starts to leave.*]

PROKHOR: [*shouts after him.*] And stop behaving as if the whole place belonged to you! It doesn't!
> [*SEMYON shakes his fist at PROKHOR and exits.*]

VASSA: Liudmila, I don't think we've met yet this morning.

LIUDMILA: No.

VASSA: And yet you haven't even the courtesy to say good morning?

LIUDMILA: [*warmly*] I'm sorry, I forgot.

PROKHOR: Good morning to you, Vassa Petrovna.
> [*VASSA avoids LIUDMILA's kiss.*]

VASSA: [*calmly, but sternly*] What do you think you've been playing at, Liudmila? Eh?

LIUDMILA: Playing at? I . . . I don't know what you mean . . .

VASSA: Go on, get out. Leave us.
> [*LIUDMILA, shocked, exits.*]

PROKHOR: Here we go . . .

VASSA: [*conciliatory*] Now then, Prokhor Ivanovich; you're an intelligent man, even a good man . . .

PROKHOR: Intelligent yes, but no more.

VASSA: Then you must at least see that your behaviour is an embarrassment to the whole family, not to mention the effect it could have on the business.

PROKHOR: Another bloody lecture. I've heard it all before from

Zahar, time after time. I told him then and I'm telling you now: it's too late to try and make me change.

VASSA: But what about Liudmila? Have you no pity for her? She's little more than a child, for heaven's sake, with all her life ahead of her —

PROKHOR: Don't try telling me about young girls; I know more about them than you ever did. And I know a thing or two about older women too, I can tell you.

VASSA: For heaven's sake, Prokhor, Pavel is your nephew . . .

PROKHOR: Yes, and you can tell him from me: if he lets that cat of his loose once more among my pigeons, I swear I'll kill him.

VASSA: You're determined, aren't you? To make the whole family your enemy.

PROKHOR: The family! Don't give me that sanctimonious rubbish! Let me tell you a thing or two about this precious family. My dear, gentle brother, your husband, was quite prepared to shove me out into the cold — and don't try to tell me you didn't encourage him. Or had you conveniently forgotten that? Some family. They've creamed off thirty thousand of mine, and that's all they're going to get. Clear?

VASSA: Then you do want to fight?

PROKHOR: What are you talking about? Fight who?

VASSA: Your nephews, I imagine.

PROKHOR: Look, you can cut out all these threats; they won't help you wriggle out of it. There won't be any fights, I can assure you. I know my rights, my legal rights, and I know what's mine. And when Zahar finally makes up his mind to die, I shall take out what I'm owed, and go. No fuss about it. Now if you'll excuse me, I must go and take my medicines. Too much exertion recently for a weak heart.

> [*He goes off, clutching his chest. VASSA follows him with her eyes, and is about to follow him when NATALYA enters.*]

VASSA: How's Pavel?

NATALYA: He's a bit calmer now. [*Pause.*] I feel so sorry for him . . .

VASSA: What did you say?

NATALYA: I said I feel sorry for him . . .

VASSA: Yes . . . He's a prisoner here. I've always felt sorry for prisoners; sometimes locked up even though they're innocent. Men used to working with nothing at all to do with their time — I feel sorry for anyone who wants to work and can't.

NATALYA: But there are people who are worse off than prisoners, surely?

VASSA: [*thoughtfully*] Nobody has ever felt sorry for me, you know. When I was over six months gone with Pavel, Zahar started going bankrupt . . . My God, we could have been put in prison, a court case at the very least. We were pawn-brokers then, and we had suitcases stuffed full of other people's things all hidden away. Of course, I could see what was going on: Zahar never intended to give anything back. He was quite ready to simply pack up and leave, if we needed to. And I'd say to him, Zahar, just hang on a little; just give me time at least to have the baby. And you know what he'd do? He'd lash out at me, yes, hit me till I was black and blue. For two whole months, I tell you, I was terrified of him.

NATALYA: Perhaps that's why Pavel was born crippled . . .

VASSA: Yes, could be, though I didn't notice he was growing up crooked until he was, oh, about five years old.

NATALYA: Tell me, Vassa Petrovna, did you talk at all with that man you got rid of the other day?

VASSA: What was there to talk about? He was useless, so I got rid of him.

NATALYA: But did you talk to him at all about . . . oh, I don't know, about life, I suppose?

VASSA: Whose life?

NATALYA: No, I mean life in general.

VASSA: Of course not. Why ever do you ask?

NATALYA: Well I did, and he said something: he said all business was . . . was sin.

VASSA: What an idiot.

NATALYA: Why d'you say that?

VASSA: I don't know — he's just clearly a fool.

NATALYA: You criticise everyone, don't you?

VASSA: So he thinks business is sin, eh? And work is sin too, I suppose. Can't you see, he's just giving himself an excuse for being bone idle. I remember once — it was before your time — there was a tramp; sat in our kitchen and preached at us, the same kind of rubbish: any work done with human hands is sinful. Right, I said, put down that bit of bread you've been given;

don't touch it, don't eat it, it's made by human hands. Put it down and clear off. And I threw him out. That showed him.

NATALYA: [*to herself*] He might have been right after all . . .

VASSA: People like that just want to complicate things. Look at Zahar: he never came out with any of that rubbish, and look where he's got to. He started out as a peasant, you know.

NATALYA: And now he's dying.

VASSA: So what? He's had a good life.

NATALYA: You've always complained about him, haven't you?

VASSA: Look: as a woman, I complain. The man's a lecher, always was. Couldn't keep his hands off a pretty girl. That's what he's dying of now. But there are other things in life than that; and there's a lot I admire Zahar for. He may have beaten me black and blue, but he's a good man really.

[*LIPA enters.*]

NATALYA: You're so inconsistent —

VASSA: No, I'm not.

NATALYA: Yes: first you say one thing, then another — [*going*] I don't understand you.

VASSA: Well, you'd do well to understand this. To Zahar and me, only one thing has mattered. Building up this business. We've worked hard at it, and nothing will get in my way now.

[*NATALYA exits.*]

Stupid girl.

LIPA: Yes, madam? You wanted me?

VASSA: Have you found out who came to see Prokhor yesterday evening?

LIPA: Yes, madam, it was somebody by the name of Eugene Mironovich.

VASSA: The solicitor from town . . . I thought so. And what did they talk about?

LIPA: I didn't hear, I'm afraid, madam.

VASSA: You didn't hear? What the hell do you mean?

LIPA:Well, they . . . they locked themselves into the room and I—

VASSA: Are you telling me you didn't even try to find out? Didn't even listen at the key-hole, for God's sake?

LIPA: But, madam, they spoke so softly —

VASSA: Damn you, you stupid girl! Why don't you do as I order you?

LIPA: Vassa Petrovna, I did try —

VASSA: Have you forgotten how much you owe me? Have you forgotten that one word from me would destroy you?

LIPA: For the love of Christ, madam, let me go! I'd go anywhere,
even . . . even to a nunnery. Just please let me go!

VASSA: Nunnery! I'll make this place into a nunnery for you, girl,
before I'm finished.

LIPA: Oh God, I can't go on any longer! [*cries*] I'd rather be dead,
I'm so frightened!
[*Pause.*]

VASSA: All right, Lipa, that's enough of all that. Come on, stop all
that noise. Here, take my hanky and blow your nose.
[*LIPA does so.*]
There, that's better. Honestly, I couldn't ever let you go, could
I? You wouldn't last two minutes out there! But Lipa, you've
got to earn your keep here. It is very important that I know
just what is going on, and I rely on you to keep your eyes and
ears open, and to let me know. All right? Now, that's all you
have to do, and I'll make it well worth your while. And do, for
God's sake, stop that snivelling.

LIPA: Yes, madam.

VASSA: Good. Now go and tell Mihail I want to see him in my of-
fice, will you?
[*LIPA exits. VASSA hears a noise at the door.*]
Pavel? Is that you?
[*The dining room door opens. PAVEL is there.*]
And what d'you think you're doing? Eh?

PAVEL: Oh, Mother . . . nothing. Nothing at all.

VASSA: What do you mean, nothing? What were you . . . oh, never
mind. Sweet Jesus, look at you. Who do you get it from, that's
what I'd like to know. Not from me, that's for sure. Idle
layabout, just like your brother — just like all of them here.

PAVEL: Well, what else can I do? I don't belong here, but I've no-
where else to go. I feel so . . . I don't know, so numb.

VASSA: Yes, I'm not surprised. Can't even keep your own wife
under control. Well, you'll just have to grin and bear it a while
longer, won't you?

PAVEL: My God, but you're a cruel woman.

VASSA: Me cruel? Ha!

PAVEL: You'd use anybody, wouldn't you? You'd use your own son
as a spade to dig the earth, as long as there were money in it.

VASSA: You know, I ought really to see you safe somewhere. Put
    you in a monastery, perhaps. Yes, you'd make a good monk.

PAVEL: What?

VASSA: Well, you're not exactly fit for anything else, are you?

PAVEL: You're serious, aren't you? My God, she's actually serious.

VASSA: And why not? Eh?

PAVEL: [*angry*] You'll never do it! You can't get rid of me like that!

VASSA: Don't you dare shout at me —

PAVEL: Let me tell you one thing, Mother. I'm not afraid of you.
    [*going*] You can threaten me as much as you want, but I'm not
    afraid.

> [*He exits. VASSA sits at her desk. She begins going
> through some papers, but her hands are shaking. MIHAIL
> enters.*]

VASSA: [*mutters*] What's the point? Who's it all for?

MIHAIL: Well? You wanted to see me about something.

VASSA: Don't take that tone with me, Mihail.

MIHAIL: What do you mean?

VASSA: It's no good you losing your temper with me. I'm still in
    charge here, my friend, so you'll just have to wait your turn,
    won't you?

MIHAIL: Oh, I don't understand anything any more. They're
    wearing me down here . . . Semyon Zaharovich just laughs at
    me . . .

VASSA: Yes, yes, all right. Listen, much more important. Were you
    aware that Prokhor saw his solicitor yesterday?

MIHAIL: Yes, I was. But that fool Lipa —

VASSA: I know. She bungled it.

MIHAIL: We must do a little reminding, I think.

VASSA: Yes . . . You see, I think she may have forgotten how fright-
    ened she's supposed to be. I'm not sure how frightened she
    really still is.

MIHAIL: Don't be ridiculous! We're talking about child murder!
    She killed her child!

VASSA: But it's dangerous for us to use that, and I think she realises
    it. After all, Semyon was the father.

MIHAIL: No, there's no proof of that. Babies don't have trade-
    marks stamped on them, after all. It was just a child, murdered
    by its mother; and we mustn't let her forget that we know.

VASSA: Will you talk to her?

MIHAIL: Maybe.

VASSA: Put the fear of God into her. It sounds better coming from a man. But be subtle about it too; we don't want to lose everything. Talking of which, I had a word with Prokhor earlier.

MIHAIL: And?

VASSA: He says he'll ruin us.

MIHAIL: And he's not joking: he would.

VASSA: Yes . . . Oh God, to lose everything now!

MIHAIL: Vassa Petrovna, we need to act, and act fast.

VASSA: [*without looking at him*] And just what did you have in mind?

MIHAIL: We only have one hope left: Prokhor's weak heart. He could go at any time . . .

VASSA: Rubbish. He'll outlive the pair of us.

MIHAIL: Well, who knows? All I'm saying is that he's taking more and more medicine with each day that passes — have you seen the size of his chemist's bills? Yakov is making a fortune out of him. And Yakov assures me that some of the medicines he's taking now are very dangerous.

VASSA: Yakov told you that? Huh, he was probably drunk — usually is.

MIHAIL: No, listen. Prokhor is taking two different kinds of medicine: one for his heart and one . . . well, I don't really know how to put this . . . one to help him keep it up . . . in bed, I mean.

VASSA: What? Dried Spanish fly, I suppose.

MIHAIL: Yes, something like that, except that the one he's taking is really powerful . . . and dangerous.

VASSA: Well, well, the randy old goat.

MIHAIL: Now Yakov was particularly worried about what would happen if Prokhor went beyond the dose he's supposed to take. You see, the two medicines don't mix at all well together, and if he were to take too much . . .

VASSA: Mihail, you're too gullible, you'd believe anything that drunken fool told you. Much more important to have that talk with Lipa.

MIHAIL: Yes, yes, of course I'll do that. But don't you see: if Zahar were to die now . . .

VASSA: [*looking straight at him*] Mihail, whatever are you saying?

MIHAIL: Me? What do you mean . . . ? I . . . I was just saying . . .

[*He tails off, embarrassed; he's suddenly unsure of VASSA's response to what he was going to suggest.*]

VASSA: [*after a pause*] You really should be more careful . . . how you say things.

MIHAIL: Yes, yes, of course. [*Pause*] You know, you gave me quite a shock then . . . quite a fright.

VASSA: No, there's nothing to be frightened of.

MIHAIL: Why, that you could even begin to think such a thing, it's . . . it's hurtful.

VASSA: I wouldn't want to hurt you. God knows, you're the only one here who really understands anything.

MIHAIL: Don't forget I've been loyal to you, I've served you well. Why, even my daughter, my only child . . . the only one apart from you I've ever cared for —

VASSA: Yes, well that's enough of that. Just thank God time is still on our side. We must just be patient. But whatever else you blame me for, you mustn't blame me for Liudmila; I know you think I arranged it, but I didn't. I was against the marriage right from the start.

MIHAIL: I know, I'm sorry, I shouldn't have said that earlier. It was that bastard, Prokhor, I know. Everywhere you go you find his grinning face leering up at you. I know what his plan was. He was too much of a coward to make the girl his mistress openly, so he marries her off to his cripple of a nephew. Christ!

VASSA: Don't put off your talk with Lipa for too long, will you?

MIHAIL: Don't worry, I'll do it.

VASSA: And do try to calm down.

MIHAIL: Yes, I'm sorry; I don't normally get so worked up.

VASSA: I know, Mihail . . . Come here.

[*MIHAIL bends down to kiss VASSA's hand and she kisses him twice on the forehead, stroking his head. He draws himself up like a soldier and exits. VASSA looks at him as he goes, then returns to her desk and her papers. The door opens softly and ANNA enters, unnoticed by her mother. She stands looking at her silently, a touch of cynicism mixed in with her affection. At last:*]

ANNA: Mama.

VASSA: Who's that — ? Why, Anna! My darling, you're here!

ANNA: And here you are, just as usual, stuck away in your office, hunting through papers. My little grey-haired Mamochka. So, how are you?

VASSA: Oh thank God, thank God you're here at last!

> [*They embrace.*]

But you wicked girl, why didn't you let us know when you were coming? I've been waiting for your telegram.

ANNA: Well, I'm here now. How's Father?

VASSA: Bad . . . Listen, did anyone see you arrive?

ANNA: A young man opened the door, but he ran away pretty quick — didn't even ask me my name.

VASSA: Hm, must have been Mitia — from the office; he's pretty vague at the best of times. That's all right then. Just let me close the door.

> [*She closes the door.*]

ANNA: So Father's no better?

VASSA: Hm? No, no, he'll never leave his bed again.

> [*She comes back from the door.*]

Good. Now we can talk without being interrupted. There's so much I have to tell you, that you ought to know . . . Well, let me look at you. My God, a real army wife, aren't you? Here, come and sit by me on the sofa. Now listen, Anna. We're in deep trouble, as I told you in my letters. It's your Uncle Prokhor. He wants to take his share out of the business. How ungrateful can you be? After all, who earned all that money for him in the first place, if it wasn't me and Zahar? Who was it who worked their fingers to the bone? And what the hell has Prokhor ever done? Fooled around chasing after women, that's all he's good for. And anyway, what does he want with money? It's not as if he has anyone to support.

ANNA: But Mama —

VASSA: No, listen. The trouble goes deeper than that. Take Semyon . . . Well, he's ruled by that pious wife of his, Natalya; she'd love nothing more than to see him get out of the business as well. And Pavel, that pathetic creature; he's married now, as you know, to Liudmila. Well, she was never right for him, it never had a chance of working. She's sleeping around now, apparently. Getting it anywhere she can.

ANNA: But that's astonishing. I'd have thought she was too squeamish for that.

VASSA: Oh, I tell you, Anna, I don't understand anything any more.

And that's why I've sent for you, Anna: you'll be able to see everything in a fresh light, see what's to be done, make sure there's not too much damage.

ANNA: I see. So what you're telling me is that we're ruined, is that it?

VASSA: I tell you, the whole business is collapsing! Thirty years of grind going up in smoke. Just like that! Hard years they were, too, with just your father and me to do it all — and it wasn't all plain sailing, either; oh no, we had our losses too. On our own, we were, nobody else to help. But the moment you're successful, out they all come creeping from the woodwork, these people who think they're entitled to a cut in the business. Layabouts, all of them. To think your father and I nearly killed ourselves for this bunch! But who can we leave it to? Who will carry it on? It took us years to build it up, and yet it's collapsing in days . . . God, it's driving me mad!

ANNA: What about Father's will? Has he made one?

VASSA: No . . . oh, I don't know.

ANNA: You don't know? You expect me to believe that?

VASSA: [*cagey*] Well . . . yes, I'm sure he has made one. It's just the thought of it: a business like this, ruined because of people's greed.

ANNA: Yes. Yes, I see.

VASSA: And there you have it. Look, will you talk to your brothers for me? They don't trust me; think I want to get control of everything. But you must make them understand, Anna; it's imperative that I keep control of all the money in the business just now, and that they don't take any of it out. They'll trust you, Annushka; after all, they know you've got nothing to gain, since you were paid your share of the inheritance when your father threw you out.

ANNA: Paid my share! Ten thousand roubles you gave me, threw it to me like you would to a beggar. And that's all I get?

VASSA: Ah, but we have the receipts, remember? Your signature that you've had your full share.

ANNA: But a receipt means nothing, surely, Mother? You'll give it back to me, won't you?

VASSA: But what will you give me in return for it? Eh?

ANNA: Give you? I'd need to know all the facts first, before I made any promises.

VASSA: Oh you will, I promise you you will. [*Pause.*] But anyway, enough of that. How are things with you?

ANNA: Oh, not too bad.

VASSA: And how's your husband?

ANNA: Him? He was promoted to Lieutenant-Colonel after the last summer manoeuvres. Got given his own battalion.

VASSA: Drinks, I suppose.

ANNA: Huh, what officer doesn't? But he — he's drinking himself into an early grave. He's already ill — he could soon be dead.

VASSA: So . . . you don't love him any more, eh?

[*ANNA does not reply.*]

Well, well, I'm not exactly surprised; and don't say I didn't warn you. But you wouldn't be told. Oh no, not you. You had to rush straight into it —

ANNA: Yes, all right, Mother. For God's sake, let's not go into all that again.

[*She lights a cigarette.*]

VASSA: Well . . . You certainly have changed. Look at you sitting there, bold as brass. Smoking too.

ANNA: So?

VASSA: Not exactly ladylike, is it?

ANNA: It suits me.

VASSA: And look at your clothes. Very smart.

ANNA: Thank you.

VASSA: And the children, how are they?

ANNA: Oh, they're well. Healthy and happy, thank God.

VASSA: But the first one died, no?

ANNA: Yes, but he . . . well, he was sickly from the moment he was born.

VASSA: I see. The first one is born weak and dies almost immediately, but after that all the rest are born healthy and strong. And this despite a husband who's a very sick man, and who, even if he wasn't sick, would be too drunk to do anything in bed except fall asleep?

ANNA: You haven't lost any of your sharpness, have you?

VASSA: And you haven't changed as much as I thought. Well my dear, so long as you're happy. And now we've got all that sorted out, I think you ought to go and find your brothers.

ANNA: Did they know I was coming?

VASSA: I didn't think that was really necessary. I wanted us to have our little talk first. Though I suspect they know now.
> [*She has gone to the dining room door, which she flings open. PAVEL is there. He hasn't had time to get away.*]

PAVEL: I couldn't hear anything, honest!

VASSA: Oh dear, what a shame.

PAVEL: Honestly, Mother, I am one of the family, you know! I heard this strange woman had arrived, with lots of suitcases, so naturally —

VASSA: You only had to knock, Pavel.

ANNA: [*comes forward*] Hullo, Pavel.

PAVEL: Can it really be? Anna, I'd never have known you!

VASSA: You ask him, Anna — why does he spy on his own mother? No, on second thoughts don't bother — I shouldn't think he has the first idea.
> [*She exits.*]

ANNA: Well . . . pleased to see me?

PAVEL: Of course. It's like living in a madhouse here.

ANNA: So Mother's just the same, eh? No change?

PAVEL: God no, she's worse. Far worse. She wants absolute control of everything now.

ANNA: Funny, I thought she had it already.

PAVEL: But don't you see? That's the point. She may have it now, but when Father dies, well — that'll be the end of it, see? I mean, there'll be Semyon and me; I'm twenty-four and he's twenty-seven. She can't keep us out.

ANNA: And how are things between you two?

PAVEL: All right, I suppose. He's a bit of a fool really . . .

ANNA: What about your wives?

PAVEL: Ah, now his wife Natalya, she's a crafty old cow, she is. Fat — and sly. And Liudmila . . . well. But anyway, what about you, eh? So smart! I wouldn't have recognised you. You look utterly different. Well, not hard to look different from people here. I tell you, this place is prison. Just look at the drab clothes everyone wears here. Grey and black. It's awful. Oh God, it's good to see you, Anna.

ANNA: And you, Pavel.
> [*They embrace.*]

Now, tell me all about yourself. So you're married to Liuda?

PAVEL: Well yes, but that's the point, you see. I'm old enough to be married but I'm still not allowed to do anything. You know, I got so frustrated that I started out on a little sideline of my own — buying up old icons from a group of the Old Believers across the river. Mother was her typical scathing self; couldn't see what I was doing, wasting a lot of money when I don't even believe in God. She'd never trust me to do anything. But I tell you, Anna, she's really missing out. Do you know, I can make ninety per cent profit on those icons? Ten roubles back for every one I pay to those monks. Antiques is good business, only she won't admit it. Why, there was one trader in town who bought six old plates for nine roubles and flogged the lot for three hundred and twenty. Three hundred and twenty roubles! And here we are wasting our time trading in bricks and tiles, peat and wood. Honestly, it's ridiculous!

    [*PROKHOR enters.*]

PROKHOR: So here she is!

    [*He stops short to inspect his niece.*]

My God, what a beauty! Here, come on, give us a kiss, then. I never could resist a figure like yours.

ANNA: For God's sake, Uncle Prokhor, don't embarrass me!

PROKHOR: Come on! Don't tell me you can be that easily embarrassed, with eyes like yours!

    [*SEMYON and NATALYA enter.*]

ANNA: [*eluding PROKHOR*] Why, Semyon. Is it? Yes, it's you. But . . . but you're so fat!

SEMYON: It is— I told you, Natalya, it's Anna! How wonderful to see you! God, how long is it since I last saw you? Must be years and years.

ANNA: And — this is your wife?

SEMYON: Yes, yes, let me introduce you. Natalya, this is Anna, my sister. Remember, I told you, the one who used to beat me up when I was a kid.

PROKHOR: Huh, she didn't make a good enough job of it, did she?

ANNA: Natalya, I'm very pleased to meet you. I hope we'll be friends.

NATALYA: Oh yes . . .

PROKHOR: Well, go on then, say something.

SEMYON: Ah well, she's the quiet type, my wife. Shy, you know. And very religious too — one of the Old Believers, all those quaint customs — christened in a cauldron and all that.

PROKHOR: Hm. Must have been a bloody big cauldron.

ANNA: And Pavel — where's Liudmila?

PAVEL: Oh, I . . . don't know, really. I think she's probably still asleep.

SEMYON: Oh yes, very likely! You remember her, don't you, Anna?

ANNA: Yes, of course I do. She was so pretty.

PROKHOR: Well, you should see her now. She looks more like her husband every day!

SEMYON: Ha! It's compliments for everybody from Uncle Prokhor today, then!

PAVEL: He only says it to annoy me . . . Go on then, all of you, laugh at me!

NATALYA: Please Pavel, please, it's all right, nobody's getting at you —

PAVEL: I tell you, they're killing me, Anna!
> [*He makes to go.*]

ANNA: Oh Pavel, don't go, please stay here!
> [*She goes after him and catches him at the door; she is trying to calm him down, but we cannot hear what they are saying.*]

PROKHOR: Quite a beauty, your sister.

SEMYON: Yes, I suppose so.

NATALYA: I don't know, I wouldn't trust her; I think her eyes are just too bright somehow.

SEMYON: Yes, she's got Mother's eyes.

PROKHOR: But what a figure, eh? And quite the *grande dame* now, isn't she?

SEMYON: And when you think of what a little tearaway she used to be!

NATALYA: I really do think Liudmila should be here; it's so rude towards Anna Zaharovna —
> [*MIHAIL enters.*]

MIHAIL: And where is she, then? Ah, Anna Zaharovna, allow me to greet you on your return to your own home —

NATALYA: [*to SEMYON*] Her own home? Surely she's been bought out of the business?

MIHAIL: [*to ANNA*] It's so wonderful to see you again, my dear, I can't tell you what a pleasure it is.

ANNA: Uncle Misha . . . Well, you haven't changed a bit, have you? I'm glad to see you.

MIHAIL: And so am I, from the bottom of my heart.

SEMYON: [*to NATALYA*] Well, what do you make of her?

NATALYA: Hmmm . . . She's a bit flashy, I'd say.

SEMYON: Oh, surely not? I mean, all her clothes are exactly the same colour!

NATALYA: Yes, yes, I can see that. It's just that —

PROKHOR: Don't know what you're both on about. Need your eyes tested, both of you. She's beautiful!

> [*LIUDMILA, enters. She has dressed hastily and looks dishevelled.*]

LIUDMILA: Oh, it's true! It's you! Anna! Oh Anna!

ANNA: Liuda!

> [*They embrace.*]

LIUDMILA: Anna . . . it's wonderful to see you!

ANNA: And you too, Liuda! But how beautiful you are!

LIUDMILA: Oh, Anna, I can't tell you how wonderful it is that you're here. A ray of sunshine in this awful place!

PAVEL: Oh God, here she goes, complaining.

VASSA: [*appearing at the door*] Anna, don't you think you ought to go and see your father?

PROKHOR: Yes, he's not at all well, you know.

ANNA: Of course, Mama, I'll go straight away.

> [*She exits.*]

PAVEL: There's no need to gloat, Uncle. You haven't got it all yet!

PROKHOR: Don't talk to me like that, you imbecile — I'll . . . I'll pull your ears off.

> [*PAVEL pulls a face at PROKHOR, who makes a lunge at him.*]

PAVEL: Don't you touch me!

> [*LIUDMILA laughs as PROKHOR begins to chase PAVEL round the room.*]

PROKHOR: Come here, you freak! I'll teach you to speak to your uncle like that!

MIHAIL: Liudmila, stop that at once. You should be ashamed of yourself. Now come here.

SEMYON: [*enjoying the fun*] Quick, Uncle, don't let him get away! That's it, Pavel, hide from him! Get under the table. Quick!

> [*The curtain falls on their grotesque chase.*]

END OF ACT ONE

ACT TWO

Evening of the same day. It is rather dark. LIUDMILA stands in front of the fireplace. ANNA, smoking and deep in thought, is pacing up and down the room.

ANNA: But I still don't understand it, Liudmila. Why didn't you ever write to me?

LIUDMILA: Well, for one thing I didn't have your address —

ANNA: Oh come on, you could have got it easily enough if you had wanted it!

LIUDMILA: All right . . . But they watch me, don't you see? Everybody watches everybody else in this madhouse, but especially they watch me — like hawks. My father, my husband . . . everyone. And anyway, what would I have written about? What here could possibly interest you?

ANNA: You could have told me about yourself — and about everybody here. You know I'd have been interested.

LIUDMILA: Oh, I don't know, it's this place, it wears you down. Over the last two years I've changed, you know. I've become so spiteful — really wanting to hurt people.

ANNA: Why, for God's sake, did you marry Pavel? That's what I can't understand.

LIUDMILA: Oh God, you think I wanted to? I had to, haven't you realised that? I had to.

ANNA: You mean — ?

LIUDMILA: Yes, I was pregnant. What else could I do?

ANNA: But . . . you were always so careful . . .

LIUDMILA: They were strange times, Anna, really strange. Nothing seemed to matter in quite the way it had before. I don't know if I can explain it . . . it was just this terrific feeling of, I don't know, I suppose of anticipation. Everything was changing, you could feel it all around you. There were riots, strikes everywhere, it seemed certain the revolution had come . . . It didn't, of course; a lot of noise, and nothing to show for it at the end. But at the time . . . well, we none of us knew where we were, and he . . . he chose that moment to come along. Oh God, Anna, he was so beautiful, so young; you could see the

scars on his face where he'd had chicken-pox before, when he was a child, but it just made him all the more beautiful to me.
[*Pause.*]

ANNA: And where is he now?

LIUDMILA: Disappeared. I don't know where he went. Just vanished one day.

ANNA: Does Pavel know about him?

LIUDMILA: No. Nobody else knows, apart from Uncle Prokhor.

ANNA: Why did you tell him?

LIUDMILA: Well . . . he helped me. At the time, I was so innocent, so worried — and he knew instinctively. I was married to Pavel, and Prokhor . . . well, he showed me how to get rid of . . .
[*She can't go on.*]

ANNA: Oh, Liuda darling, I had no idea!

LIUDMILA: But that boy, oh, he was so gentle and kind. He may have looked ugly to other people, what with those scars on his face, but to me he was beautiful. And so good to everyone . . .

ANNA: Yes, of course. But Prokhor! Tell me about him, Liuda. I feel I scarcely know him.

LIUDMILA: Oh, he's all right. He's fun to be with — not boring like most of the traders around here. And I know you won't believe this, but he can be gentle too — no, don't laugh, it's true! He'll be tender, loving . . . mind you, there are always strings attached! Oh yes, I soon found that out. If he helps you, then you give him what he wants — and you'd better be good. Nothing comes free! Not here. Still, why should I complain, eh? He did me a good turn once, didn't he? And we aren't paupers — we must pay our debts. No, it's only fair I should still have to pay.

ANNA: Yes, I suppose so.

LIUDMILA: There's only one person I feel really close to, and that's your mother. But I hardly ever get a chance to talk to her properly. She never asks me anything. Once in a while she'll give me a lecture about Pavel, but that's about it . . . And yet, and I know this sounds funny, but I honestly feel she's the only one who is really sorry for me, and who really understands me and loves me. Honestly! I don't think I could have gone on without her.

ANNA: Really?

LIUDMILA: It's so hard to explain. But . . . well, now the summer is here we'll work together in the garden, your mother and I. I love that, being with your mother. She'll knock on my door really early; and you know that gruff way of talking she has, well she'll just call out, "Liudmila, get up!" And we'll go out . . . and work. We don't talk at all, but we're together. And I love it. I love that garden. I've learned so much there. It's the only place I can feel any, oh, self-respect, I suppose. Your mother understands that. She gave me a book once, about gardening. "Here," she said, "read this. Learn all about it, gardening's an honest profession." I'm really at home in the garden, planting and weeding . . . and grafting. Oh yes, I'm really good at that! Why, the peasants in the village come out here and take lessons from me. Yes, truly, from me! They respect me. And out there I can respect myself. It's the winter I hate. And your mother does too, I can tell. Locked up in this awful house, suffocating to death. I tell you, there's no room to breathe here. Your mother and I . . . well, we don't say much to each other but I know we can both of us feel it. Stifled. Anyway, that's enough about me. What about you, Anna? You look so miserable all of a sudden.

ANNA: Just remembering this place. Can't help being sad. Oh look at you, you're so young, so beautiful!

LIUDMILA; Oh, I just get carried away when I talk about gardens. It's my only true passion in life. Honestly!. I go out there in the morning and — well, I feel drunk, I'm so happy. I just want to sing. And when I stop singing your mother is always there, and she shouts out, "Go on, sing!" She looks so funny, stuck behind a shrub, shouting out — but her face then, it looks so gentle, so kind.

ANNA: Gentle and kind! My mother? Oh come on, Liudmila, never could you say —

LIUDMILA: Oh, but you can!

[*PAVEL enters quietly.*]

Don't you remember when we used to play in the garden — ?

PAVEL: And what are you two gossiping about?

[*He lights the candles on the table.*]

LIUDMILA: Nothing that would interest you. Oh, why must you light those candles!

PAVEL: The better to admire you, my dear.

LIUDMILA: Put them out.

PAVEL: No.

LIUDMILA: Please!

PAVEL: What, and not be able to see my beautiful wife?

LIUDMILA: You have to ruin everything, don't you? Reduce it all, destroy it.

PAVEL: Well, Anna, you see what kind of creature they've chained me to, for the rest of my life.

LIUDMILA: Chained you! You liar! You crawled to me, on your hands and knees, cringing like some beggar —

ANNA: Oh stop it! Stop it, both of you!

LIUDMILA: Anna, don't you see? He's incapable . . . of anything. So he gets at me in different kinds of ways, nasty, sordid little ways. Do you know, just to get at me he killed my cat. A Siberian tom-cat, a beautiful animal, and he poisoned it.

PAVEL: The bloody thing bit me, scratched me. And anyway, I didn't poison it — it ate itself to death!

LIUDMILA: Oh, shut up, just — do you know, I can't even bear to look at you now. You disgust me.

[*She exits.*]

PAVEL: [*after a pause*] Well, you heard that, did you, Anna? I disgust her. She can't bear to look at me.

ANNA: Oh, Pavel, what can you do?

PAVEL: Nothing. Oh, I'm well aware of that. I'll suffer on — but by God, I'll make her suffer too! Anna, for the love of Christ, help me! I'll give you anything you want, money, my share of the business, anything, everything, only help me! Help me!

ANNA: Pavel, what is it? How can I help you?

PAVEL: Teach her to love me, for Christ's sake. Oh, Anna, I love her so much. You married for love, didn't you, so you know what it's like.

ANNA: Yes, I suppose I do.

PAVEL: Do you know, at night I kneel by her bed when she's asleep, just looking at her and thinking, knowing that nobody, nobody will ever love her, could ever love her as much as I do. I'm there sometimes all night, whispering to her right through the night, "Liudmila, my darling, I need you, everybody needs something; look at me, a deformed cripple, I have nothing to live for except you and I need you . . ." And she . . . she doesn't

wake up. She doesn't know how much . . . Oh, Anna, for pity's
sake, help me!

ANNA: Pavel, please, please calm down. Somebody's coming,
they'll hear you.

PAVEL: I don't care, let them all come. Let them all know —

[*NATALYA enters.*]

NATALYA: Ah, Pavel, I've been looking for you. Vassa Petrovna
wants you.

[*She looks suspiciously at PAVEL and ANNA.*]

I should go to her quickly, she's in a foul mood.

PAVEL: Huh, she always is.

NATALYA: Please, Pavel, she wants to see you. It's about one of the
office boys — he's been complaining about you.

PAVEL: All right, all right, I'll go.

[*PAVEL exits.*]

ANNA: Natalya, just a moment, don't go.

NATALYA: Yes?

ANNA: Poor Pavel. You know, he's completely drained me.

NATALYA: What, complaining about his wife?

ANNA: Yes, that above all, I suppose . . . You get on with him, don't
you?

NATALYA: I like to think I get on equally well with everyone.

ANNA: Really? Doesn't that make life a little . . . I don't know, a
little boring for you?

NATALYA: Why should you think that?

ANNA; Well, put it this way. You're young and — well, there's not
a lot here to interest you, surely?

NATALYA: What about my husband?

ANNA: Ah, Semyon, yes — but is that enough? Honestly?

NATALYA: Semyon Zaharovich tries very hard to make life here
amusing for me. He likes telling little jokes, as you well know.
And anyway, I wouldn't have thought these were necessarily
times when one wanted too much frivolity.

ANNA: Why do you say that?

NATALYA: Well, don't you see? Everything is going to change! We
can't go on living as we have been. The whole of our society
is about to be completely altered. We — that is people like us
— we need to move from here, into the towns.

ANNA: Into the towns? What on earth do you mean?

NATALYA: I can't explain it very well, though I think about it all
the time. But — well, these have been terrible years, years of
riot and unrest. We need to get everything firmly under control once more, the towns and cities need to be completely
under the control of the army and the police, and that is where
we need to live, in cities where order has been restored. We
are not safe at the moment, Anna. Everybody talks in whispers,
we're all too frightened to speak out; and strange people are
wandering the countryside, going from place to place . . . Do
you know, there was one here not long ago, he tried to per-
suade us that we should do nothing, that all work was sinful! I
can tell you, he frightened me, and he's been on my mind ever
since. Just imagine what would happen if everyone thought
that, and nobody worked any more! We must have order, I tell
you!

ANNA: You really have thought about all this, haven't you?

NATALYA: I can't help it. I don't sleep well anyway — worse than
usual at the moment because one of the children is ill — and
so I lie awake thinking, trying to work it all out. But nobody
ever listens to me; they all think I'm too young to say anything
that matters.

ANNA: Well, I've listened to you!

NATALYA: Yes, I know, and thank you.

[*PROKHOR bursts in.*]

PROKHOR: Where the hell's Vassa?

ANNA: Oh, Uncle Prokhor, I don't know, I'm afraid.

NATALYA: She's got Pavel with her, in the office.

PROKHOR: So, plotting again. The bitch! She won't get away with
it!

ANNA: What are you so angry about now?

PROKHOR: Listen. My pigeon loft. It's filthy. For three months
I haven't been able to get up there to clean it. And why? Because they won't mend the ladder, that's why. And that's not
accidental, I can tell you. Oh no! If I were to fall off I'd go
head first into the cellar and break my neck. Yes, it's all part
of her plot. Her and that twisted brat of hers, Pavel; it would
be all part of his sorcery.

ANNA: Uncle, you don't know what you're talking about!

PROKHOR: Oh yes I do! You don't know what goes on around
here. So, today, I do get up there — I have to, damn it, after

that cat got in there. And while I'm up there, someone very quietly opened the trap door down into the cellar and moved the ladder to the very edge. It was dark, I couldn't see a thing, and the floor was damp . . . I tell you, I'm bloody lucky to be alive now. So how do you explain that, eh? Which of these criminals was behind that one, do you suppose?

NATALYA: I've said it before: Pavel can only take so much. If people carry on getting at him, it might drive him to do something really desperate. I've told Liudmila that as well.

PROKHOR: You see, Anna? Even Balaam's ass here agrees with me.

NATALYA: Really, Uncle Prokhor, I'm a merchant's daughter —

PROKHOR: I tell you, it was Pavel!

ANNA: Natalya, really, why do you support him in his wicked ideas?

NATALYA: He can't hide his wicked thoughts. He's unhappy, that's what makes him so spiteful.

PROKHOR: My God, d'you hear that? Butter wouldn't melt in her mouth . . . but I tell you, Anna, she's dangerous, this woman. Got the instincts of a snake. Am I right, eh, Natalya? Rattlesnake Natalya! Go and rattle somewhere else!

NATALYA: You're a cruel man, aren't you? I feel very sorry for you.
[She exits.]

ANNA: Honestly, Uncle, why must you be like that with her?

PROKHOR: Oh, don't you worry yourself about her; she can take it all right. I tell you, I don't trust that pious soul in her black dress. You know, I heard her once — she didn't know I was there — I heard her talking to Semyon about the next world. [imitates NATALYA] "And there I'll be, Semyon, wearing my mauve velvet dressing gown with nothing on underneath it but my lace night-gown — "

ANNA: Good God, Natalya?

PROKHOR: Yes, I tell you! "Lying down or sitting on my *quelque-chose* — "

ANNA: Don't you mean chaise-longue?

PROKHOR: How the hell do I know? "And these people will come to see me, the police chief, the mayor, the judge — the whole town, in fact! And d'you know what, Semyon? They'll all be so envious of you when they look at me. And I, I'll just tease them, won't I? Just let my night-gown slip a bit over my shoulder, accidentally reveal a bit of leg, and then see them sweat — " My God, I bet they would sweat too! What a disgusting picture, eh? Semyon, of course, well, he just laughs, that dirty little snigger of his.

ANNA: She's a strange woman, though. You know, I can't make her out at all. She seems somehow, I don't know, simple, terribly naive . . . She was saying some very odd things just now.

PROKHOR: Devil knows what she's really like. I don't care. The way she rolls those great moony eyes of hers — Anna, she's like the rest of them in this madhouse. I tell you I'm fed up with the lot of them.

ANNA: Then why on earth do you stay?

PROKHOR: I've got no choice, have I? All my money is here, thanks to Zahar, tied up in this blasted business — and that means Vassa's got it really. I can tell you, the moment I've got my money I'm off — finished with all my oh-so-loving friends and relatives.

ANNA: And where will you go then?

PROKHOR: Me? I'll go to Moscow, to the capital. Where, as I may as well tell you, I have certain ties. The . . . how shall I put it . . . well, the product of a rather unfortunate love affair lives there, growing up now, and growing up rather well, I must say.

ANNA: Really?

PROKHOR: Yes, quite grown up and very handsome. A student he is, very clever. Quite a lad, in fact. I'm proud of him.

ANNA: And what about his mother?

PROKHOR: Ah . . . she died, alas. But the boy — well, he calls me his "unexpected" father. Cheeky little sod. But he never asks me for anything, not a thing. Not like people around here. No, a good lad. Drinks a bit too, goes to the theatre a lot, got to know all the actresses, the devil. He's at the University: studies mythology.

ANNA: Philology, surely?

PROKHOR: No, don't you try and get all clever with me. Mythology, that's what he's studying. He told me all about it. Got me quite interested in it, he did. All about the Greek wars, that *Iliad* thing. I'm reading about Odysseus at the moment, as it happens. What a crafty one, eh? Wonderful liar, he was. Said he'd been down to hell and, well, it wasn't that terrible or frightening at all, no, the only thing was, it was very, very boring. How d'you like that, eh? Now that Piotr of mine, he's a pretty good liar too, you know.

ANNA: Yes, I'm sure!
         [*VASSA enters.*]
VASSA: What on earth have you been saying? Eh? Which one of
    you has upset Natalya?
ANNA: Why? What has she said?
VASSA: She's standing there in the middle of the dining room,
    tearing her handkerchief to pieces — she's absolutely white
    with anger! Honestly! [*to PROKHOR*] Anyway, Prokhor, that
    pigeon-fancying friend of yours wants you.
PROKHOR: Huh, he can wait.
ANNA: [*keen to get her mother to leave*] Is Semyon back yet?
VASSA: [*suspicious*] Why?
ANNA: Well, didn't you want to see him?
VASSA: What? Oh, I see. Yes, I do. I'll go and look . . .
         [*She exits.*]
PROKHOR: Old misery! [*to ANNA*] What about a game of cards,
    eh? We'll call Liudmila —
ANNA: Yes, if you want. But what were you saying about getting out
    of the business?
PROKHOR: I must, Anna; I'm getting too old for it. Anyway, it's
    not like it used to be any more. Oh no; I tell you, I get fright-
    ened sometimes. Everything is changing here, Anna, every-
    thing. Time was, you'd walk through the village and you'd feel,
    well, like one of the gentry, almost; you know, respected. Now
    . . . well, they may still be bowing when you go past, but that's
    only to hide their faces, so you won't see the anger written
    there. Well, I ask you, what kind of a life is this? It's each man
    for himself now, grab what you can and sod the lot of them
    . . . just like that *Iliad* I was telling you about. Anyway, I've never
    exactly been much of a businessman, and I can't really see why
    I should bother with it now. No, the moment Zahar's gone,
    I'll get my money, then off to Moscow, to Piotr.
    [*SEMYON enters; he's been out, so is wearing his coat.*]
SEMYON: Someone wanted me?
ANNA: Yes — Mama.
SEMYON: Funny, she said it was you! Good — nobody wants to see
    me. Thank God!
PROKHOR: Semyon, what about a game of cards? I'll fetch Liuda.
SEMYON: All right, why not? Honestly, life in town is so much bet-
    ter than life here. Wonderful; solid. Houses made of stone,

the whole place is light and clean, and the people — well, they're different from the people here, all right. Interested, they'll talk about anything, they know so much more . . . and then there's the Douma, so all kinds of political talk, political views — there's just so much going on!

PROKHOR: [*as he goes*] Yes — and so much coming off, eh?

SEMYON: Prokhor, you lecher!

[*PROKHOR exits, laughing.*]

ANNA: Look, Semyon, I'm worried. Do you think, honestly now, that Prokhor is playing around with Liudmila?

SEMYON: Playing around? Oh, that's good. Playing around. Yes, I was wondering how you'd phrase it. I like that. That's what I mean about living in a town; you learn how to say things.

ANNA: Yes, all right, but . . . well? Is he?

SEMYON: Well, of course he is! How naive can you be! And not just "playing", I can tell you. My God, I heard him once, giving her what I suppose you might call a lesson. Taught me a thing or two, anyway. The mind boggles.

ANNA: Such as?

SEMYON: I couldn't possibly say.

ANNA: Oh, come on, I am a married woman!

SEMYON: As if that made any difference! And anyway, I didn't really follow all of it. Something about how to stay . . . well, you know . . . safe . . . children, and all that. That sort of thing, as well as — but anyway, forget Prokhor. He's just a spoilt child, really. He gets bored, has to have things to amuse him. The business isn't enough to keep him going.

ANNA: And you?

SEMYON: Me? Well, let's face it, bricks and tiles and peat don't exactly make for an interesting life, do they? And anyway, it's all different now. The men are so sullen, somehow. Have to keep calling in the police, they're always drinking and fighting. I'm sick of it. The moment Father dies, I'm off. I'll go and live in town. It's better there; so many more people around. Here . . . well, you're so exposed, aren't you?

ANNA: And who do you suppose will run the business?

SEMYON: I don't really care, to tell you the truth. It'll just have to be cut back, won't it? There's no profit selling peat, anyway. No, Mother and Mihail can look after it. Me, I'll be off into town. I'm going to open a jeweller's shop, right there in the

main street, right in there with the gentry. And there'll be a
sign up there: "Semyon Zheleznov, Jeweller". Jeweller, eh?
Sounds good, doesn't it? And I'll have a flat over the shop and
— I think I'll buy a harmonium and learn to play it.
                    [*LIUDMILA enters.*]
LIUDMILA: Anna, Semyon, quick, for God's sake, try and stop
    them!
SEMYON: Who? What is it?
LIUDMILA: It's Uncle Prokhor and Pavel, fighting again!
SEMYON: There you are! Now you see why I want to escape from
    this place and get into town for a bit of peace and quiet. Well,
    go on then, Anna, what are you waiting for?
ANNA: Me? Why should I go? You're the man here, you go and
    break it up. Anyway, they might hit me instead.
SEMYON: Oh, all right. But I'm not a blasted policeman, for
    heaven's sake . . .
                    [*He exits.*]
LIUDMILA: Oh God, Anna, I can't go on, I really can't. It's just
    wearing me down, living here like this.
ANNA: Calm down, Liuda, it will be all right in the end.
LIUDMILA: I wish Prokhor would kill Pavel. Oh, of course I should
    feel sorry for him, but I can't, Anna. He's so — repulsive.
ANNA: How did this latest one start?
LIUDMILA: Pavel said he wouldn't let me play cards with you and
    Prokhor. Honestly, Anna, most of the time it's so pathetic I
    just have to laugh at him.
ANNA: And?
LIUDMILA: It's understandable, given . . . well, everything, that
    Prokhor should have that effect on him. Something just cracks
    in him, and he goes wild . . . Suddenly he's shouting at me,
    pushing me around. So in goes Prokhor, fists flailing. I tell
    you, it's so ridiculous — but it's awful, Anna, to see them brawl-
    ing like this!
ANNA: Yes, brawling just like the peasants they like to think they're
    superior to. It's terrible you should be forced to live here,
    amongst these people.
LIUDMILA: Oh no, Anna. Everything in life has to be paid for, as
    I said. And so now I'm paying for those moments of happiness
    I had. I think back a lot these days, remembering — it helps
    to take some of the pain out of living here. Remembering him

there before me, crying for sheer happiness, both of us so happy, so dear to each other, so blind . . . you do know what I mean, don't you?

[*ANNA embraces LIUDMILA.*]

ANNA: Yes . . . yes, I know what you mean, Liuda.

LIUDMILA: And at that moment — well, you're rich, aren't you? I mean, there's nothing that matters any more than that feeling. No regrets, you feel so full you'd be happy to die then and there . . . yes, I often think back to that.

[*VASSA enters.*]

VASSA: What's all the noise?

LIUDMILA: Oh, Mama, can't you do something?

VASSA: Why, what have you done now?

LIUDMILA: Nothing. It's Pavel and Prokhor — they're fighting again.

VASSA: Again? Oh, Liudmila, I did ask you —

LIUDMILA: I can't! You must see that, Vassa Petrovna; I cannot pretend to love a man I hate! You know it yourself; when it's that strong there's nothing you can do to deceive him — nothing!

VASSA: Your problem, Liudmila. You deal with it. You'd better go and find them and calm them down.

LIUDMILA: But what, please, what am I supposed to do?

VASSA: You must find the answer to that yourself, mustn't you? We all suffer, and we all have to learn. Now go.

[*LUIDMILA exits.*]

ANNA: And how long has all this been going on, eh?

VASSA: Oh, I don't know. Two years, perhaps three . . . a long time. Sometimes, I tell you, I feel so sick of the whole lot of them, I'd like to get rid of them all, just be shot of them. But it's Pavel I feel sorry for, Anna. He has the worst of it.

ANNA: Pavel? He doesn't exactly make life easy, does he? Especially not for Liudmila.

VASSA: Oh, she can take it — and she deserves it, too!

ANNA: What is actually going on between her and Uncle Prokhor? Do you know?

VASSA: Oh yes, I know all right; I know all about that bastard Prokhor! He found out Liudmila's guilty secret — you knew about that, didn't you? Yes, I thought so. Well, he found out, and

he's taken advantage of it — and taken advantage of her. You
know, he's an animal, that man.

ANNA: Look, we must have a proper talk, you and I, Mother. I'll
come in and see you when you're in bed.

VASSA: Why? What is it? Don't tell me you've got some bombshell
to drop too!

ANNA: No, Mother, it's just that I think we ought to have a little
talk. I don't know why it is — probably just that I'm an out-
sider — anyway, I had them all trooping up to me all evening
and baring their souls.

VASSA: What? Prokhor as well?

ANNA: Yes, him too. Tell me, did you know he had a son?

VASSA: Huh! Be a miracle if he had only one!

ANNA: That's as may be. But were you aware that there's a special
one — a boy that it wouldn't surprise me if he adopted?

VASSA: [*jumps up*] No, you're lying, aren't you? You're trying to
put the wind up me. Well, Anna?

ANNA: That's what he said . . .

VASSA: But that — that means the end, for all of us! If he adopts
a boy, then what happens to the property if he dies? It goes to
the son! I can't bear it! Oh God, is this what I've been working for, building up this business for this? He can't do it, he
mustn't!

ANNA: And of course, Semyon's desperate to get away from here
and set up in town.

VASSA: I see. And what else did you discover this morning? Any
other little titbits?

ANNA: Pavel's not happy here either; he's longing to leave as well.

VASSA: Right, that's enough. I'll look after him, find him somewhere to go. Oh yes, I can see what you're driving at. Learning all our secrets, so you can move in for the kill. And what
about me, eh? Decided where I'm to be put, have you?

ANNA: Mother, no, you haven't understood —

VASSA: Oh yes I have, I understand you well enough. And you can
just watch out, or —

[*There is the sound of people approaching noisily.*]

God, what now?

[*PROKHOR, SEMYON and NATALYA enter excitedly.*]

SEMYON: Stop it, Natalya, for pity's sake!

PROKHOR: Will somebody get rid of this silly girl! Shut her up!

NATALYA: No! It's time somebody here told the truth for once. And who will do it if I don't?

SEMYON: Natalya, Natalya, not now, my darling, my precious little one, not now. Look, I promise you, soon we'll be away from all this in town, remember? And the sign, yes? J for jeweller? So not now, please? Choke it back, eh?

VASSA: What in God's name is going on? What are you all doing in here?

PROKHOR: What is going on? Well, your precious daughter-in-law Natalya has chosen this moment to fly into a rage with me. With me!

NATALYA: Yes, with you! You're the one, with your taunts and your insults, who has driven poor Pavel almost out of his wits!

PROKHOR: Semyon, for God's sake do something with her, or I swear I'll —

ANNA: Uncle, please, you're supposed to be the one in the family with a clear mind —

PROKHOR: Clear mind! I've been driven out of my mind long ago living here. Do you know what Pavel did? He drew a knife and threatened me. Threatened me, he did! He wanted to kill me!

[LIUDMILA enters quietly and sits in the corner, watching carefully, but unobserved.]

NATALYA: But you're to blame for it, Prokhor, don't you see that? You're to blame for all of this.

VASSA: Semyon, have you no control over your wife?

SEMYON: Oh yes, that's what you want, isn't it? Everything under control, eh, Mother? But you'll see one day, Mother — you're driving us all away and there'll be nothing left to control!

NATALYA: I must speak! For once the truth must be told! It was you who ruined Liudmila.

PROKHOR: You idiot! She was shop-soiled long before she got married, before I knew her. I — well, go on, Anna, you tell them. You know all about her, don't you?

[LIUDMILA has risen and come forward.]

LIUDMILA: No, you tell them, Prokhor. Go on, tell them all. Long before I was married . . . Well?

VASSA: Liuda, stop it, for God's sake! What on earth has come over you?

PROKHOR: Oh damn you all to hell, the lot of you! And as for you, you . . .

LIUDMILA: Yes? What's holding you back?

PROKHOR: Just you wait! I'll make you shut your mouth!

LIUDMILA: Not frightened, are you? Uncle Prokhor, got cold feet!

VASSA: Liudmila, stop it!

LIUDMILA: Oh come on, what does it matter now! What does anything matter? Pavel is going to find out now, isn't he? Going to find out everything!

SEMYON: Natalya, please, come with me. Please, before you say anything else.

LIUDMILA: Natalya here, our little saint, she'll never keep her mouth shut now, will she?

NATALYA: And why should I? The truth! That's all I want. You're just frightened of hearing the truth!

SEMYON: Natalya, just remember — we'll soon be away from all this. Now please, come with me.

NATALYA: Very well — but remember, you cannot hide from the truth, any of you!

[*SEYMON and NATALYA exit.*]

LIUDMILA: Oh God, if only I could escape from all this! Just clear out and go far, far away and never come back!

VASSA: Well, there you are, Anna, there's our family for you. No loyalty in any of them. Just out for all they can get — just grab and run!

LIUDMILA: No, no, Vassa Petrovna, don't you see? I don't want anything from you — just my life! For God's sake give me my life!

[*PAVEL enters.*]

PAVEL: Mother, help me. Give me my money, my share of the estate —

VASSA: You see what I mean? Another one — just grab, grab, grab.

LIUDMILA: Oh Pavel, look at you! And your head, still bleeding.

PAVEL: Mother, you must help me. As a mother you must see — Anna, tell her. For pity's sake tell her to let me go, let me get away from here!

VASSA: Oh, I'll find somewhere for you to go soon enough, Pavel.

ANNA: Mother, please, you must see it makes sense. You must let him go now, far away. Can't you see? Prokhor is capable of anything!

PAVEL: No — no, I'm not afraid of him.

ANNA: Look at the state Pavel is in now — Prokhor did that to him.

PAVEL: No, that's not the point, Anna!

ANNA: I know Pavel's not strong, but even a weak man, if he's tormented far enough . . . I tell you he could do anything.

VASSA: Nonsense.

LIUDMILA: Anna . . . What are you saying? Why, it's almost as if you wanted Pavel to kill him.

VASSA: That's enough, all of you! Liudmila, go now, leave me with Anna. I need to talk to her.

LIUDMILA: Very well, if that's what you want.

VASSA: And you too, Pavel. Go with Liudmila. I'll come and see you both later.

> [*They go. VASSA paces up and down then stops in front of ANNA.*]

So . . .What's the plan, eh? What little scheme are you cooking up?

ANNA: I . . . I don't know what you mean.

VASSA: Oh come on, I wasn't born yesterday. And Pavel is my son — or had you forgotten that?

ANNA: I honestly don't know what you're on about!

VASSA: Don't lie to me! I can see right through that pretty little head of yours. You wind your brother up until he kills Prokhor, and then you can step in, can't you? Scoop the lot! Very clever!

ANNA: Mother! That's a disgraceful thing to say! I never —

VASSA: And you come out the winner, don't you! You beat all of us.

ANNA: I never even —

VASSA: You think you're pretty clever, don't you? Well, you haven't beaten me yet, and I promise you, you never will! Never!

> [*A knock.*]

Who is it?

> [*MIHAIL enters.*]

VASSA: What now? How's Zahar?

MIHAIL: Bad. His breathing's getting worse and worse.

VASSA: Oh, if only God would take him now! Five weeks he's been like this, suffering terribly. Gasping for breath. And yet — he's still conscious, still understands everything that's going on around him. If only he could be released from his suffering!

MIHAIL: But the end can't be far off now.

VASSA: No . . . I must go to him. Wait for me here.

[*She exits.*]

ANNA: It's a terrible life you're all living here, Mihail Vassilyevich.
I'd no idea things were so bad.

MIHAIL: Bad! I swear to you, things couldn't be worse. I don't
know where we are — everything's in a complete muddle.
Everything.

ANNA: How on earth will it all end?

MIHAIL: I don't know, I really don't know . . . I can't believe, somehow, it will ever end.

ANNA: It's so hard for Mother, just keeping things together. Uncle
Prokhor doesn't help, either.

MIHAIL: Him, help? Prokhor? He doesn't know the meaning of
the word.

ANNA: And does that surprise you?

MIHAIL: No, not at all. You see, Prokhor has discovered the great
trick that Russian men are always playing. Prokhor is a fool at
heart. But where he's clever is in persuading people that all
the time he's acting according to his conscience. So he can
pour scorn on your mother and me, you see, because he's always hiding behind his bloody conscience. Very cunning.
He's trouble, all right.

[*LIPA enters.*]

All right, Lipa, don't just loiter there. What do you want?

LIPA: It's a message for Anna Zaharovna . . .

ANNA: Well?

LIPA: It's your Uncle Prokhor, madam. He wants to see you.

ANNA: Have you any idea why?

LIPA: I think he's not feeling well . . . it's his heart.

ANNA: His heart? What's she talking about, Mihail? Is something
going on?

MIHAIL: Oh, it's nothing to get worried about. He's had this
trouble before.

LIPA: He gets breathless, and then —

MIHAIL: Yes, breathlessness . . . Lipa here knows all about it, don't
you, Lipa? Well go on, Anna, if the old man wants you.

ANNA: Yes, of course.

[*She exits.*]

MIHAIL: No, not you as well, Lipa. You and I must have a little
word.

LIPA: What about?

MIHAIL: Oh come on, Lipa, you know perfectly well what about.
Don't try to fool me. [*Pause.*] Well?

LIPA: I won't do it. I can't.

MIHAIL: Why not?

LIPA: Because I'm afraid. Please, I'm terrified.

MIHAIL: Why? Because you think it's a sin?

LIPA: But of course it's a sin! He's a human being, for God's sake!

MIHAIL: And what about your own child, eh? Wasn't that a human
being? Wasn't that a sin, then? To throttle your own child —

LIPA: Stop it! Please, stop it!

MIHAIL: With your own hands, you, the mother, to strangle your
own child, and you talk to me about sin!

LIPA: Yes, all right! It was my child, and I murdered it! I killed my
child out of pity, because I couldn't bear to think it would be
brought up in this foul place!

MIHAIL: That may be. But you're not exactly out of danger yet,
are you? Prokhor knows all about your guilty secret —

LIPA: So what? You do too, only too well. Does that mean I'm supposed to poison you as well as Prokhor? Well? Am I to kill you
too?

MIHAIL: [*trying another, gentler tack*] Shush, you mustn't get so
worked up, people will hear, and we don't want that, do we?
Now listen, it could be so easy, just a little accident, anybody
could do it. You mustn't be afraid, Lipa. Do it now and everything will be fine, I promise. Now is the perfect moment for
it! Take both the bottles of medicine, and pour him a double
measure — if he asks about it you can always tell him that that's
what the doctor said we should do if he had another attack —
but he won't ask, I promise you! And anyway, this isn't poison,
is it? It's medicine. Remember that. And then when it's done
you can go from here, wherever you like, we won't stand in
your way any more. You'll be free, at last, and you'll be able to
forget about the past.

LIPA: Please . . . please don't make me do it . . .

MIHAIL: Listen. You want to be free, don't you? Free of us, free
of the past. Well then, there's only one way. Remember what
the Old Believers across the river say: there can be no salvation
without repentance; and there's no repentance without sin.
Nobody can get through this life without sinning, Lipa, nobody. And that's all we're asking you to do now. One last sin,

and then you'll be free of us forever. You can go with God's
blessing — and I can promise you, we'll show our gratitude as
well. You'll be able to live the life you want to. You're young,
you shouldn't be shut up here. You've got to escape somehow.
And the only way out is to do what I say. Well?

LIPA: You're evil, aren't you? All of you! Oh yes, I'll do it. I've got
no choice, have I? Dear God, you'd use anybody to get what
you really wanted.
                [*She exits.*]

MIHAIL: More conscience, more rubbish like that. Can't she see
the sort of world we're living in? Scruples . . . that's just crap.
You've got to act, and act decisively . . .
                [*The door opens; PAVEL is there.*]

PAVEL: Where's Mother?

MIHAIL: Gone to Zahar Ivanovich.

PAVEL: Who were you talking to?

MIHAIL: Nobody . . . myself.

PAVEL: Huh, some companion. Make sure he doesn't swindle you.

MIHAIL: Thanks for the advice. I'll take it as a reward for all I've
done for you in your miserable life.

PAVEL: Take it how you like — I couldn't care.
                [*PAVEL goes. MIHAIL shakes his fist at him, and then
                starts to pace up and down. VASSA, SEMYON and NA-
                TALYA enter.*]

VASSA: Well, Mihail, it looks as though this really is the end for
Zahar.

MIHAIL: [*under his breath*] And Prokhor is far from well.

VASSA: Yes, it can't be long now. Semyon, you'd better go into town
and fetch Father Yegor back for the last rites.

SEMYON: Very well, Mother. [*to NATALYA, softly*] Here we go
then, my love; it's all beginning to break up quite nicely! Just
remember that sign, up there in the main street in town: "J"
for . . . all right?
                [*He exits.*]

VASSA: Natalya, what was he saying to you? Something about —

NATALYA: Oh nothing, Vassa Petrovna, nothing at all. In fact, I
didn't really hear what he said.

VASSA: Oh really . . . Well, I wish to God you'd stop following me
around like this. Every time I look round, there you are, brood-
ing away. Look, why don't you go to your room, or something?

NATALYA: But I can't.

VASSA: Why ever not?

NATALYA: Because I'm afraid, Vassa Petrovna.

VASSA: Afraid of what, for God's sake?

NATALYA: Well, I can hear Zahar Ivanovich next door, fighting for his breath, and it frightens me.

VASSA: Oh, don't be so stupid. There's nothing to be frightened of. Honestly! Look, Zahar is very ill, I know that; and he's going to die soon, very soon now. Well, there's nothing we can do about that; we must all die some time. For heaven's sake, I'm much closer to death than you are, and I'm not afraid, am I?

NATALYA: No, of course not, Vassa Petrovna.

VASSA: So there you are then. Now, go along with you, and leave me here with Mihail. There are some affairs about the business that I must discuss with him in private.

NATALYA: Of course. I'm sorry if you think I've been intruding . . .
  [*She exits, wrapping her shawl about her.*]

VASSA: Honestly, that woman. She's frightened, is she? Well, she's not too frightened to be eating me out of house and home. The amount she puts away! Anyway, enough about her. What were you saying about Prokhor?

MIHAIL: Yes . . . I rather understand that he's had a little recurrence of his heart trouble. Lipa has just gone to give him his medicine. I . . . I tried to impress upon her how dangerous the wrong doses could be to a man in Prokhor's state of health, and how important . . . well, how important it was that the right decisions be made for all our sakes.

VASSA: I see . . . And did she understand what you were saying to her?

MIHAIL: Oh yes, I think we can safely assume she got the drift.
  [*LIPA starts screaming, in the dining room.*]
  Dear God — that's Lipa —
  [*ANNA rushes on.*]

ANNA: What is happening in this house? This is madness!

VASSA: What are you talking about?

ANNA: Lipa . . . she's poisoned Uncle Prokhor!

VASSA: Poisoned! And is he dead?

ANNA: No . . . that is, I don't think he is. Lipa is just standing there and screaming.

VASSA: Mihail. You must do something quickly.

MIHAIL: Yes, let me think ... Not dead, you say? Well, the police, then. We must call the police.

VASSA: No, we must think. Anna, where are you going?

ANNA: I must get back in there! Lipa —

VASSA: Will you stop fussing! We must be calm, all of us.

ANNA: But she's in there, screaming her head off!

VASSA: Then, Mihail, you must go and bring her in here.

ANNA: But she needs a doctor too; the girl's hysterical!

VASSA: No! We will sort it all out in our own way, without —

[*LIPA enters.*]

LIPA: Oh, Miss Anna, help me, please help me! Whatever shall I do?

VASSA: So . . . here you are. And what in God's name do you think you've done now, you wretch?

LIPA: Madam, please, it wasn't me, it wasn't my idea! Mihail said —

VASSA: Shut up! I don't want to hear any excuses. After all, it's not as if it's the first time you've given Prokhor his medicine. Don't you know the proper dose?

LIPA: For God's sake, let me go from here. Please!

VASSA: Go from here! And it might even come to that! Or perhaps you aren't aware that you can be put in prison for making the sort of mistake you've just made. How on earth could you mistake the doses like that, I just don't understand it.

LIPA: Mistake? But I thought . . . What's going to happen to me? What are you plotting for me now? I did what —

MIHAIL: You fool. Just wait till I —

VASSA: Now that's quite enough! Shut up! Lipa, get in there, and wait for me there. Go on, girl, move! Mihail, for God's sake get her out of here now!

[*LIPA and MIHAIL exit.*]

Well, and what's wrong with you, Anna? Cat got your tongue? And don't look at me like that! Listen, the girl made a mistake, that's all; she gave him the wrong dose. Could have happened to anyone. Oh, I know I was a bit hard on her, but that's because I was so shocked. I mean, it could have been dangerous. But after all, it's quite understandable. The house is in uproar, your father is dying. Lipa's left on her own to look after everything, it's not surprising she makes a mistake . . .

ANNA: [*quietly*] Oh no, it's not surprising at all, Mother. I see exactly what you mean.

VASSA: I don't know what you mean by that . . . but all right. Then you should understand this. What goes on here, the way I have to run things, is no concern of yours — clear? It's none of your business. So don't try to come over all high and mighty with me. Now, go and make yourself useful; go and see to your uncle.

[*NATALYA enters.*]

NATALYA: Vassa Petrovna, Anna, come quickly, please! Uncle Prokhor —

ANNA: What, is he dead?

NATALYA: Oh Anna, what an idea! Why —

VASSA: Yes, Anna, what on earth could give you such an idea? Eh?

ANNA: Nothing, Mother. Nothing at all, I assure you. It was just the way Natalya came in —

VASSA: Well, I'm sure there's nothing to worry about. After all, he had two heart attacks in the winter. Mild ones, I know, but he got over them all right.

NATALYA: I know, but he gave me such a scare. I heard this noise, and I went into his room — and there he was, writhing on the ground, groaning, great gulps like . . . like hiccoughs, I suppose —

VASSA: How awful, yes, just think of it! And yet you know, when I get hiccoughs after dinner, nobody feels worried about my health, do they? Still, there we are. Now go along, both of you, for God's sake. Go and look after Prokhor.

NATALYA: Very well. Come along, Anna.

[*NATALYA exits.*]

ANNA: My God, Mother, you frighten me. You know that? You're so calm, so cold . . . yes, you frighten me all right.

[*She exits.*]

VASSA: Oh, Anna, if only you understood! Now then, where is she? Lipa! Mihail! Come in here!

[*MIHAIL and LIPA enter.*]

You stupid girl! He's alive! D'you hear me? Alive! We trust you, and you bungle it! Dear God, I could strangle you! Go on, get out of my sight! I never want to see you again!

MIHAIL: You'll pay for this, I promise you!

VASSA: No, leave her alone, Mihail. She's not worth it.

LIPA: Vassa Petrovna, I don't understand. I did what I was told to!
    It was Mihail, he told me to do it!
VASSA: Get out! Do you hear me? Go to your room, now!
LIPA: Please believe me; it wasn't my fault! I only did —
VASSA: Go!
LIPA: Oh, dear God, help me, help me please . . .
                    [*She exits.*]
VASSA: So . . . you bloody fool, Mihail!
MIHAIL: All right, so I was wrong.
VASSA: And that chemist you put so much faith in!
MIHAIL: Yes, all right! Something went wrong. I'm sorry . . .
VASSA: Sorry! And to think I trusted you on this one. What the
    hell do we do now? Right, first things first: Lipa. You must
    keep a close watch on her. She must not be allowed to get word
    of this to anyone, got that? No one at all.

END OF ACT TWO

ACT THREE

Several days later. VASSA sits by the hearth, dressed in mourning. ANNA, also in mourning, paces up and down, smoking. SEMYON is also there.

SEMYON: Anybody else want some tea? It must be time by now, surely!

VASSA: No; we haven't been back from the funeral for forty minutes yet.

SEMYON: Oh damn the forty minutes! Father wouldn't have minded. I don't give a damn about this forty minutes thing. Why should we all have to sit around here with long faces?

VASSA: Semyon, stop throwing your weight about and try to behave yourself for once.

SEMYON: Look, I'm bored. My wife's not feeling well, and I'm not allowed to do anything; can't play cards, can't go out, can't even have a cup of tea! And it's not just the hypocrisy of the thing; it's enough to make you stagnate, just sitting around here!

VASSA: Your father only just dead and buried, all you want to do is to go off and enjoy yourself! Honestly! You know as well as I do, we must mourn your father for forty days —

SEMYON: God! Forty days, forty minutes, and then we can become human again! I mean, look what this place is doing! Natalya's all worked up, her nerves —

VASSA: Huh! Natalya's nerves! I can't think what she's complaining about! I'm forty-eight and there's never been anything wrong with my nerves!

ANNA: [*throwing her cigarette on the fire*] Yes, but you're exceptional, aren't you, Mother? I know what Natalya means. This place is getting to me, too. The house, you know . . . it's full of strange noises, strange echoes . . .

VASSA: Rubbish, it's just the rats. Rats and Prokhor's damn pigeons, most likely.

ANNA: No, I can hear this creaking in the night —

VASSA: Just the floor-boards drying out after the winter —

ANNA: And shadows. Everywhere I look I get the feeling there are shadows moving around, following me.

VASSA: Yes . . . must be Lipa's ghost.

SEMYON: Oh Mother, for heaven's sake, why do you have to bring all that up now!

VASSA: Pacing up and down, up and down . . .

ANNA: I never thought you'd believe the ghosts of suicides come back to haunt the living.

VASSA: I don't know. Why not, for God's sake? She had cause enough.

SEMYON: Oh no, Mother, all you ever believed in was hard cash.

VASSA: Semyon, you're an idiot, so I won't take offence at what you say. And anyway, talking of hard cash, who do you think your father and I built it all up for, eh? For our children, of course. And look at you! Not worth a single rouble. Why you, Semyon, you couldn't even give me a grandson, you're so useless.

SEMYON: You lying —

ANNA: Semyon, for heaven's sake!

SEMYON: I gave you a grandson!

VASSA: Yes, by a serving girl!

SEMYON: So what? I had a son. What does it matter who the mother was? And anyway, you needn't sound so high and mighty; you laid her on for me in the first place.

VASSA: In any case, it doesn't matter, given that the poor little thing was born dead, not healthy at all. You see, Anna, Semyon is lying about that —

SEMYON: [*jumping up*] My God, Mother, you'd lie your way out of everything, wouldn't you? He wasn't born dead. I know that now. Lipa told Natalya everything. It was Lipa herself who . . . God help her, who killed our son. He was a perfectly healthy boy, and she strangled him. And then you found out, didn't you, Mother? And you blackmailed her with it, made her life a misery, until she couldn't bear it any longer. That's why she hanged herself, Mother, because of you. You killed her!

VASSA: There, Anna, see what I have to put up with.

ANNA: Semyon, how can you say such foul things about Mother! Awful things.

VASSA: No, Anna, you're a mother too, you'd better find out now what it's like to have an ungrateful child!

SEMYON: I can see it all now, Anna, oh yes, sucking up to Mother. You don't want to hear the truth about her, do you? Well, let me tell you something, my precious sister, it won't do you any good. You'll see!

[*He exits.*]

VASSA: So there you are, then; how d'you like that?

ANNA: Do you know, I don't think I've had any idea how hard it must have been here for you all these years. I just didn't realise . . .

VASSA: Ah well! Thank God for my thick skin, eh? I can take it. But I'm glad you're beginning to understand . . . God knows, I need somebody here who does.

ANNA: But aren't you frightened at all? I am.

VASSA: What d'you mean?

ANNA: I mean I'm frightened for you.

VASSA: Huh, there's no need to be. I can outwit this lot.

ANNA: I think I still have a lot to learn.

VASSA: We're all learning all the time. Me too! My mind's constantly full of things, problems, complications, endlessly; no solutions, just questions, endless questions. Have you ever thought about why it is that grown men behave as though their mothers had nothing to do with them, that it was their fathers alone who begat them? Well, if you haven't noticed it yet, just hang on a bit, you will. That business with Semyon just now, and Lipa . . . well, I saw the look you were giving me.

ANNA: And?

VASSA: And it's true, of course it is. All right, I wanted to look after him, he was so unhappy, pining away, and so I let him carry on here with Lipa. And now he flings it back in my face! And then, when he's tired of Lipa, he goes off and finds someone else in the town. Who then, mind you, gives him a dose of the clap.

ANNA: [*quietly.*] But is it really true — what he said about the child?

VASSA: And what if it is? Eh? What else was I supposed to do?

ANNA: I don't know . . . I just don't understand how you could . . .

VASSA: For God's sake, don't you start judging me as well! Listen, you'd do the same in my shoes, I promise you! You wouldn't let some other woman's child live off what you've carefully saved up for your own family, worked so hard for!

ANNA: No, perhaps not . . . I don't know. But that reminds me. There was something I'd been meaning to talk to you about. You know I told you about that boy of Prokhor's in Moscow?

VASSA: Well? What about him?

ANNA: Prokhor has written to him. Twice now. He's given me the
letters to post. [*Pause.*] He's asking the boy to come here.

VASSA: But this is awful! This means another —

ANNA: Precisely. Another vulture wanting his share of the corpse.
But — I didn't post the letters.

VASSA; You didn't? Thank God for that.

ANNA: No, and I don't think they should be posted.

VASSA: No, of course they shouldn't. Oh, you're a clever girl, Anna,
cunning, yes, you take after your mother. You and I, we'll look
after this home and this business . . . So! How much do you
want for the letters?

ANNA: Mama, really, how could you?

VASSA: One hundred roubles the pair. A fair price?

ANNA: Honestly! Just take them! How could you suppose I wanted
to sell them!

VASSA: All right, all right, no offence meant. I'm a mother, like
you, and as a mother I'm prepared to stoop to anything to
preserve my family. Remember, for the sake of your children,
in their interest, nothing is shameful, nothing is ever a sin. So
don't try and get all moralising with me; I know my standards,
and I'll never be ashamed!

ANNA: You know, you're really quite remarkable! Here, here are
the letters.

VASSA: Thank you. Yes, all mothers are remarkable. We're great
sinners all right, but by God we're martyrs too. I may have a
lot to answer for at the day of judgment, but before man I shall
never repent. Remember, we, the mothers, gave life to everything. And when I get to that judgment seat, I'm not worried,
the Holy Mother of God, she'll understand, she's a mother too.
She pities us sinners — why, she even asked the Archangel if
she could go into the deepest hell to comfort the very worst
sinners! Oh, she'll know why I did all the wicked things I've
done in my life; I've fought as a mother has to fight, and as only
a mother knows!

ANNA: You know, when I arrived back here, I thought I was better
than you; more cunning, cleverer . . . But now —

VASSA: Ah, that's enough of all that. You think what you like about
me, I don't care. But I'll very soon tell you if you're wrong, remember that!

ANNA: All right. But listen, those letters. Uncle is getting better all the time, so he'll write again, and then post them himself — or get me to send them registered post and give him the receipt.

VASSA: That's not a problem. I've got drawers full of old post office receipts. Mihail can just alter the name and the town and so on, and then stamp it. Easy. I used to do it all the time when your father was carrying on with his tarts over in the town. But you must make sure Prokhor gives the letters to you — no one else.

ANNA: Of course.

VASSA: Liudmila, for instance, she's only a child, he might well get round her.

ANNA: I'll take care of that. I don't think they're exactly fond of each other at the moment, and anyway, she tells me everything.

VASSA: But this business with Prokhor is so important. We've just got to stop him taking his money out, otherwise there'll be nothing left for your children.

ANNA: Mother, really, you know that's not —

VASSA: I know nothing of the sort! Look, you can't fool me, and why should you? Haven't you heard what I've been saying? We're both mothers, we'll fight . . . You can't fool me, I can see right through you.

ANNA: Yes, all right. You don't mince words, do you?

VASSA: Life's too short. Speak your mind, that's my motto — and you should be honest with me.

ANNA: D'you know, I don't think I've really understood you before now. All right then; as one mother to another, we must help each other.

VASSA: Yes; I'm your mother, and God help me, I'll be a mother to your children too.

> [*The door to the dining room opens slowly and NATALYA enters.*]

Whatever's wrong with you? You look as if you'd seen a ghost!
> [*She laughs.*]

NATALYA: I'm sorry — I thought we'd been called for tea, but now I can see . . .

VASSA: If you want tea, you'll have to lay it. Where's Liudmila?

NATALYA: Uncle called her.

VASSA: Did he? I see.

[*She signals ANNA to leave them, but ANNA doesn't see.*]
Anna, go and ask Prokhor if he wants some tea.

ANNA: Yes, of course, Mother.
[*She exits. VASSA watches NATALYA for a moment.*]

VASSA: Are you feeling any better then, Natalya?

NATALYA: I don't know . . . It's awful, I can't sleep, I'm so upset. And on top of everything else, Kliamzinsky's wife came to see me.

VASSA: She's wasting her time, I tell you.

NATALYA: But she keeps on crying and crying —

VASSA: Huh, that won't help. Tears won't even get a face cloth clean.

NATALYA: But Vassa Petrovna, could you not pardon him, in memory of the deceased —

VASSA: The deceased no longer has anything to do with the business — and you'd be better advised to stop meddling in it yourself! All right?

NATALYA: [*angry*] It is just possible that I really do feel sorry for these people!

VASSA: Sorry! What on earth is there to be sorry about? If he was too bone idle to work, he doesn't deserve any pity. After all, what did you do when you had a lazy nanny? You sacked her on the spot!

NATALYA: Maybe. But that was because of my child!

VASSA: And this is because of my children! I'll fight for this business any way I can, but to do that I need good workers. What kind of a mother, let alone a boss, would I be if I filled the place with drunks and layabouts?

[*VASSA exits. NATALYA waits, disconsolate, and is about to leave when PAVEL lurches in. He has a glass in his hand and is rather drunk. He sits down heavily.*]

NATALYA: Watch out, you'll spill it — Heavens, what a mess! Are you drunk, Pavel?

PAVEL: No, not drunk, just slightly — shall we say merry? Eh?

NATALYA: [*cautiously*] Liudmila . . .

PAVEL: [*quickly*] Yes?

NATALYA: She's . . . she's made it up with Uncle, you know?

PAVEL: Yes . . . yes, I know.

NATALYA: Oh Pavel, I do feel so sorry for you.

PAVEL: Ah, you're always feeling sorry! What good has it ever done?

NATALYA: Pavel, we're so alike —

PAVEL: Why — you a cripple too? I'd no idea!

NATALYA: I mean we're both clever — and our fates are the same!

PAVEL: You clever! Could have fooled me.

NATALYA: No, seriously, Pavel. Your mother — well, she was here just now. She thinks I'm a fool, I should have no say in anything. But really now I'm the master's wife, aren't I? Zahar Ivanovich is dead, and so Semyon is head of the family. And yet — she treats me as though I were a servant!

PAVEL: I don't give a damn!

NATALYA: But Pavel, don't you see, we're the same, you and I, and we need to act! We're not given our freedom, are we?

PAVEL: Don't I know it! But that's all over now. I'll soon show them who I am. I'll go away from here — get into town, into Moscow, anywhere. Sod the lot of you. I don't want you, this house, this business, any of it. I've had enough, I tell you, enough!

[*SEMYON bursts in with DUNYA.*]

DUNYA: Please, Semyon Zaharovich, please — don't hurt me!

SEMYON: Look what I've caught! A bloody little spy! Standing out there listening to everything. Weren't you?

[*DUNYA screams.*]

NATALYA: Oh yes; Vassa's little sneak. Telling her what we say, eh? Everything gets back? Well, that'll all change now, I can tell you.

SEMYON: What were you doing behind that door?

DUNYA: Nothing, Semyon Zaharovich, I swear it!

PAVEL: Go on, hit her! If she won't tell the truth, hit her!

DUNYA: No! Help! Pavel, no, please! I wasn't doing anything!

PAVEL: Liar! You lying bitch! Tell us what you were doing!

DUNYA: I . . . I heard talking — that's all, I couldn't hear anything, I swear it, not one word . . . and I was just waiting — I didn't want to interrupt anything —

PAVEL: Ah, you can't fool me.

SEMYON: No, you can't fool him — he's the champion spy himself!

PAVEL: Watch it, Semyon, or I'll sock you one too!

[*PROKHOR enters, supported by ANNA and LIUD-MILA.*]

NATALYA: Uncle Prokhor, whatever are you doing out of bed? You look awful!

PROKHOR: What's all this noise, then? Who's screaming?

NATALYA: It's Dunya — she's been spying on us. But Uncle, quickly, sit down!

LIUDMILA: Semyon, leave her alone, please. Oh, how you all enjoy tormenting people!

NATALYA: Meaning you don't, I suppose?

PROKHOR: Now, now, no quarrelling please!

SEMYON: So, how are we going to punish this little sneak?

PAVEL: Let me get at her, I'll break her lovely little nose for her . . .

LIUDMILA: No! You can't!

SEMYON: No, I've a better idea. Here, Natalya, go and get the oil from underneath the icon. I think she ought to drink it.

DUNYA: No! Please!

PAVEL: Yes — good idea. Go on, Natalya. Then we'll see her —

ANNA: [*sternly*] Leave her alone, Semyon.

SEMYON: But —

ANNA: That's enough! Now Dunya, go. Nobody will hurt you now, I promise.

DUNYA: Thank you, thank you, Anna Zaharovna.
[*She exits.*]

NATALYA: And just who do you think you're talking to? You're not in charge here, you know.

PAVEL: Ah, what's it matter who's in charge? None of it matters — it won't be long now.

SEMYON: Yes, Anna, what do you think you're doing, bossing us about?

PROKHOR: Oh, well said — standing up for yourself at last! Him, the oldest! Ha, wet behind the ears!

PAVEL: Don't you start. I tell you what, though, I'll get those dirty stinking pigeons of yours before I go — I'll put the cats in there and then we'll see!

ANNA: Pavel, stop it! Don't annoy him. Can't you see — ?

PAVEL: Who d'you think you are?

ANNA: I'm your older sister and I'm telling you —

PROKHOR: Don't, Anna, just leave him to me. I'll make him —

SEMYON: Anna, you have no right to talk to us like this!

NATALYA: Yes, my dear sister, I'm afraid you are no longer one of us.

PAVEL: I tell you, it doesn't matter! None of it will last! None of it!

SEMYON: Listen, Anna, you've had your share of the business, remember? You aren't going to get any more; you've had your lot. Clear?

PROKHOR: God, if it's like this now, Zahar scarcely cold in his grave, whatever will it be like in a week? What'll happen then?

LIUDMILA: Nothing will happen. Nothing will ever happen.

PAVEL: I'll tell you what'll happen then! I'll send the lot of you to the devil, all of you! I'll get rid of the lot of you. And especially you, you old lecher!

PROKHOR: You watch it, you drunkard. Watch that tongue of yours.

PAVEL: Ah, shut up!

ANNA: Uncle! Pavel! Both of you, stop it! Pavel, you should be ashamed of yourself! Can't you see how ill Uncle Prokhor is? Heavens, if you carry on at him like this he might well have a relapse — anything might happen!

PROKHOR: Anna, don't tell him that! You'll just make him worse.

ANNA: It's very dangerous for Uncle Prokhor to get all excited. Why, the slightest thing could give him another heart attack, and the doctor said the next one — well, it could well be fatal! And you wouldn't want to have his life on your hands, would you?

PROKHOR: Anna, for heaven's sake!

LIUDMILA: Anna, you mustn't!

PROKHOR: He'll just do it on purpose!

ANNA: Now you mustn't get all worried, Uncle; that's almost as bad.

NATALYA: Really, Anna, talking to him like that! Anybody would think he was a criminal! How dare you treat him like that!

PROKHOR: And who asked you, eh? Since when were you mistress of the house?

[*VASSA enters in a hurry, with MIHAIL.*]

VASSA: Semyon! This business about Kliamzinsky the salesman. Did you give the orders to reinstate him?

SEMYON: Yes, I did. After all, he's a good worker. Drinks a bit maybe, but there's nothing so terrible in that, is there?

VASSA: Oh, isn't there? The wife, I suppose, put you up to this?

SEMYON: No, no, Natalya has nothing to do with it.

VASSA: Really? I was referring to Kliamzinsky's wife — but your answer is rather more revealing!

LIUDMILA: Let the cat out of the bag there, Semyon!

PAVEL: Don't you start.

NATALYA: It's all right, Semyon, I've already told Vassa Petrovna —

VASSA: Yes, and I've already told you, and I'll tell your brainless husband too. This business is not yet yours to do with as you please. I'm in control here still. And Kliamzinsky goes. Clear? Good.

PROKHOR: Oh dear, I don't envy you, Vassa. What a time you're in for. I feel quite sorry for you.

VASSA: Why, thank you, Prokhor. But don't forget to keep some of the pity for yourself.

PROKHOR: Yes, what a fix you'll be in, eh? With this lot fighting it out. Whoever said Russians were supposed to be gentle and kind, eh?

NATALYA: I hope you're not suggesting, Uncle, that any of us is wicked?

PROKHOR: Who, me?

NATALYA: Really!

LIUDMILA: [*to ANNA*] Well, Anna, you're very quiet. What do you say? Are we wicked?

ANNA: I don't know.

LIUDMILA: I think Natalya's right. Nobody here is wicked.

PROKHOR: Oh? Well, you might be right, I suppose —

LIUDMILA: [*overriding him; passionately*] No! Not wicked! Just terribly, appallingly unhappy. Unhappy because nobody here has any idea how to love anything.

PAVEL: That's a lie for a start!

SEMYON: [*to NATALYA, who is about to speak*] No! "J", remember? Say nothing.

LIUDMILA: [*over the others*] Unhappy because they can't tell the difference between good and evil.

PROKHOR: Yes, well, you're right there. They haven't the first idea.

VASSA: And you, Liudmila? If you're so clever? I suppose you know what matters, what's good, eh? You know how to love?

MIHAIL: Careful now, Liuda —

LIUDMILA: Yes I do, I honestly think I do. Shall I tell you what is right and good? Your garden. That's where the truth is. I've loved it since I was a child, and I love you, Vassa Petrovna, because you've made that garden so beautiful.

VASSA: [*touched, despite herself*] Yes, well, perhaps . . .

LIUDMILA: I'm often terrified of you, of course —

MIHAIL: Liudmila!

VASSA: No, let her finish.

LIUDMILA: Don't worry, Papa. Because then I look at the garden and think of you bent over, working among the apple trees, picking the fruit, the flowers — and I see that you know as well as I do what is good and evil. You know — and nobody else here has the slightest idea.

PROKHOR: Well, assuming that —

SEMYON: [*as before*] Natalya — "J"!

LIUDMILA: They'll never know. Never. It's a foreign country to them.

NATALYA: Taken to prophesying, have you?

PROKHOR: I know what this is all about; she's after something!

SEMYON: Yes, you're right! And Anna too! The two of them making up to Mother, oh yes, both in it for themselves!

VASSA: Really, Semyon? You know, you're a big boy now. You really ought to try and keep your thoughts to yourself.

NATALYA: He's not afraid of you any more —

SEMYON: "J"!

VASSA: What's that silly thing you keep saying?

SEMYON: Oh, nothing, Mother, nothing at all. Just "J". Nothing really.

[*VASSA makes a despairing gesture.*]

PROKHOR: Well, don't stop there, Liudmila. Tell us something else we don't know.

LIUDMILA: What's the use?

VASSA: No, you don't need to. You're a good woman, Liudmila. May God bless you with good children.

LIUDMILA: By him? Not much chance of that, have I? Not much chance of healthy, normal, good children fathered by that cripple!

[*There is a shocked silence.*]

NATALYA: Oh!

MIHAIL: Why, you wicked girl!

PAVEL: [*picking up a paper knife from VASSA's desk*] I'll kill you! I'll —

VASSA: No Pavel, stop!
          [*She knocks the knife from his hand, and restrains him.*]

PAVEL: Let me go, Mother! Let me get at her!

VASSA: No.

PAVEL: You're on her side, aren't you? You're my mother, but she means more to you than I do. All of you here, in this room, you none of you care about me, do you? Family! This is no family! In a family people are supposed to love each other! But look at you all. Uncle? Wife? Brother? I hate you all! And you, Mother, are you really a mother to me? You won't give me my share of the money, you won't let me go — I hate you all! I'll — I'll burn the place down!

ANNA: Pavel, please, don't say —

PAVEL: Don't come near me! You're just as bad! What good are any of you to me?

VASSA: Dear God! What good are you to any of us?

PAVEL: You torment me! You hunt me like a wild animal, like a pack of dogs! Why? Oh God! Just give me my share of this place and I'll go, Mother, I swear I'll go!

VASSA: Your share? And just what is that, eh? What belongs to you here?

NATALYA: But everything here belongs to Semyon and Pavel now! Can't you see that?

ANNA: Shut up, Natalya!

NATALYA: You're finished, Vassa Petrovna, finished!

ANNA: Natalya, for God's sake, shut up!

NATALYA: Another one can't face the truth, eh? I'll speak my mind!
          [*VASSA strikes NATALYA.*]

VASSA: You bitch!

NATALYA: Oh!

SEMYON: Mother!

NATALYA: You won't get anywhere by calling us names, Vassa Petrovna! We're not children any more, and we'll fight for our rights if we have to!

VASSA: Oh yes? Fight, will you? Well, let me tell you —

ANNA: Mother, I really think you should —

PAVEL: Yes, fight for our rights! For my rights! I'll fight.

ANNA: Pavel! Can't you see how ill Uncle Prokhor is looking?

PAVEL: Yes, and I'll finish him off now once and for all!

PROKHOR: What? Anna, for God's sake, help me!

ANNA: Just a moment, Uncle, I'll get something for you. [*to VASSA*]
Mother. Come here. Quickly.

VASSA: What — ?

ANNA: Just come! I must talk to you.
[*They exit together.*]

SEMYON: [*as they go*] Mother, you really can't treat us like this.
We've had enough of it, all of us —

PROKHOR: Liudmila, please, for the love of God, help me. I feel
terrible.

VASSA: [*from the door*] Liudmila, come here.

LIUDMILA: But we can't just —

VASSA: Now! At once!

ANNA: [*offstage*] It's all right, Uncle, I'm coming.

PAVEL: [*yelling*] I'm the master here now, I tell you. Me: the
cripple. And I hope he dies —

ANNA: [*offstage*] Pavel, leave him alone!

PAVEL: — I hope you all die!

PROKHOR: So that's what you really want, is it? You want to kill
me! And he means it — by God, he's gone mad. Mihail, help
me, help me get away from him!
[*He tries to get up from the chair.*]

PAVEL: Yes, I'll kill you all right!
[*He makes a rush at PROKHOR. MIHAIL, who has apparently gone to help PROKHOR get up, in fact holds him
down in his chair. NATALYA catches PAVEL before he
gets to PROKHOR, and restrains him.*]

NATALYA: No, Pasha, stop — please!

MIHAIL: It's all right, Prokhor, now don't worry yourself.

SEMYON: Pasha, stop it. Mihail, for God's sake get him away from
here. He's gone berserk. Mother — quick! Come here!

PAVEL: I've wanted to do this for a long time, Prokhor; ever since
you first ruined my life — and I'm not going to be stopped
now!
[*He manages to get free of NATALYA and SEMYON and
attacks PROKHOR, punching him in the chest. PROK-
HOR tries to rise, but again MIHAIL, under the guise of*]

> *helping him, in fact holds him back in the chair. PAVEL
> kicks PROKHOR before being pulled off by SEMYON and
> NATALYA in the general melee. He slumps to the floor,
> sobbing. PROKHOR has collapsed in the chair. ANNA
> rushes on with a bottle of medicine.*]

ANNA: What in heaven's name has happened here? Uncle!

> [*VASSA and LIUDMILA follow her. VASSA goes to
> PAVEL. MIHAIL crosses to LIUDMILA and takes her
> aside, as ANNA forces pills down PROKHOR's throat —
> more than the permitted dose, which nobody can see.*]

SEMYON: Let's go out of here, quick!

ANNA: I warned you, Pavel. Heaven only knows I warned you . . .

NATALYA: No, wait —

PAVEL: Get away from me, Mother!

ANNA: Water! Quick, get me water!

MIHAIL: Are you listening to me?

LIUDMILA: How can I? Now? Tell me later, can't you?

ANNA: Water, somebody, now!

LIUDMILA: Here.

> [*She breaks away from MIHAIL, picking up a cup and
> taking it to ANNA, who gives it to PROKHOR to make
> him swallow the pills.*]

MIHAIL: Shouldn't we get him to his room?

LIUDMILA: But we can't move him —

ANNA: No, Mihail is right. We'll take him upstairs. Mihail, help
me.

> [*MIHAIL helps ANNA to lift PROKHOR and carry him
> out. As he does so he mutters:*]

MIHAIL: Well, well, Prokhor. That girl Lipa may have messed it
up, but I won't. I hope you can hear me. This is for my
daughter, Prokhor, and for the business.

> [*They exit.*]

NATALYA: I'm frightened, Semyon. There's something going on
here. Did you see how they egged Pavel on deliberately?

VASSA: What are you hissing about?

NATALYA: Hissing? I'm not a snake.

VASSA: All right — what did you say, then? Eh?

NATALYA: Now, listen Mother —

VASSA: What were you saying?

NATALYA: We're in charge now, don't you see? You can't order us around as if we were your servants any more.

VASSA: [*very quietly*] Get out.

NATALYA: [*almost hysterical*] Don't you raise your voice at me! Semyon, tell her not to shout at me.

SEMYON: [*trying to speak with authority*] Now look here, Mother, that's enough! I'm twenty-seven and Pavel's twenty-four — we're not children any more, you know.

> [*From outside we hear the distant sound of what is in fact PROKHOR's last struggle in which MIHAIL's hand is injured, but it is so distant as to be quite indistinct. VASSA pushes her glasses onto her forehead and stares straight at SEMYON, without speaking.*]

Why are you staring at me like that? Look, whichever way you look at it, it's the law, Mother; we're of age and . . . well, we're the sons and heirs . . . You can't argue with the law, Mother!

VASSA: [*turning at last to PAVEL*] Go and see how Prokhor is.

PAVEL: No. Please don't make me. I can't.

SEMYON: That's right. You can't force us to do anything from now on.

VASSA: Oh dear. You were born a fool, weren't you, Semyon?

SEMYON: That's enough! First you insult Natalya and now — well, I won't stand for it. A fool I may be, but I also happen to be the master now. So please —

> [*ANNA enters.*]

ANNA: Mama, you must come quickly. I think Uncle Prokhor is dead.

> [*LIUDMILA gasps and rushes from the room. Silence. PAVEL sits down, holding his head in his hands. SEMYON blinks, unable to believe it, while NATALYA clings to him. VASSA crosses downstage, but says nothing. ANNA watches her closely.*]

SEMYON: [*at last*] My God, I can't believe it.

NATALYA: [*slowly realising*] The estate — yes, of course! Don't you see? Now it's all ours!

ANNA: For God's sake, Natalya!

VASSA: [*turning slowly to PAVEL*] So, Pavel, you got what you wanted in the end.

PAVEL: Please, no, I — I was drunk, I didn't know . . .

SEMYON: Oh, Pavel, what have you done?

[*VASSA and ANNA exit, but ANNA pauses at the door.*]

NATALYA: [*crossing to PAVEL*] Pasha, tell me the truth. Did they put you up to hitting Prokhor?

PAVEL: Oh no, please, please, no. I can't have . . .

SEMYON: What are you trying to say, Natalya?

ANNA: [*hastily re-entering*] Oh, Pavel, and after all I said to you. I warned you, God knows I warned you often enough not to touch him.

NATALYA: Yes . . . Of course, you weren't egging him on, were you? I mean, it just so happened that . . .

PAVEL: It's not my fault, I tell you! It can't be!

NATALYA: God will judge the guilty ones. He knows who they are.

> [*MIHAIL enters with a handkerchief hastily wrapped around his hand. VASSA and LIUDMILA follow. LIUDMILA crosses the room and sits in the corner, quietly weeping.*]

PAVEL: I was drunk, I tell you I didn't mean . . .

SEMYON: How — I mean . . .

MIHAIL: It was the blow he got, he must have . . . well, his heart, you know. We tried everything, but . . .

NATALYA: [*softly*] His hand . . .

ANNA: [*sharply*] What's that?

NATALYA: Mihail's hand . . . it's bleeding.

MIHAIL: Oh, that? Yes, I knocked it against the door, carrying him out. It's just a scratch. But thank you for your concern, Natalya.

VASSA: So. What now? Liudmila, for God's sake, stop crying. That won't help us now. What are we going to do with you now, Pavel? [*Pause.*] God knows, this family is hardly a united one, scarcely happy. But if rumour of this were to get about outside . . .

PAVEL: What are you saying?

VASSA: [*unemotional*] It could be a police affair. There's money involved, after all. More than a hundred thousand, Prokhor had in the business. He wanted to take it out — well, we all knew that. But that makes . . . complications. You can see that? And we warned you not to touch him, even the slightest excitement could kill him. But you — you deliberately . . . Are you aware of what you've done?

PAVEL: Don't torment me! No — no, you wouldn't! You wouldn't tell! You're my family, please . . . Mama! You can't! Semyon, help me!

VASSA: Yes, we're your family, and we'll stand by you. In public. But how can you be at peace with yourself? No, Pavel, I have thought about this. The best thing for you is to go and live in a monastery.

LIUDMILA: In a monastery?

PAVEL: No, you can't! I won't go! Semyon, help me! I won't do it!

VASSA: I'll make a large donation to the monks, and you'll live there, quietly. You'll be out of all harm. You'll learn to pray — to pray for yourself, and to pray for us.

PAVEL: Look — look at Liudmila! She's glad! She's beaten me! Liudmila, please, I beg you . . . No? No pity? My God, Mother, what a wife you found for me!

VASSA: No, Pavel, you wanted her.

MIHAIL: Yes, you did.

VASSA: Remember how you threatened to kill yourself?

NATALYA: Yes, I remember that.

VASSA: You keep out of this! So, Pavel. Give me your promise. You'll go into the monastery. It will be best for you — best for everyone. No one will laugh at you there, you won't be mocked for being a cripple. I will know that my son is safe at last, at peace. You see that, don't you? Well, think it over — until tomorrow. Tomorrow you will agree to go.

PAVEL: Happy now, Liudmila? I shan't forget this. Smirking at my downfall . . .

LIUDMILA: No, Pavel, not at your downfall, at my freedom. Pavel, if there is a drop of humanity in you, let me go, for Christ's sake. I shall always speak well of you, I promise; when I think of you, I swear it will be with tenderness in my heart. The only one here to think of you like that — except your mother. But don't you see, Pavel, you must let me go? Especially after today — you must . . . Please, Pasha dearest, let me go!

PAVEL: Don't! Don't talk as if you cared for me! Yes, I'll go, but don't pretend you care.

LIUDMILA: Thank you. Thank you, Pasha.

> [*She goes over to him and kisses him on the forehead, without touching him otherwise.*]

PAVEL: Dear God. You even kiss me as though I were a corpse. No
— no, I see this, it's a conspiracy, isn't it? You want to get shot
of me so you can get my money! All this stuff about prison,
police — lies! Monastery! No, I'll not go quietly into some
monastery where you can forget about me! I'll go, all right,
but you must give me my money, my share. I'll get rich then,
I tell you, rich, miles away from you all — and when you come
begging to me, I'll set the dogs on you! You hear me? I'll look
out of the window and see the dogs chasing you away, tearing
at you! So give me what I'm owed!

VASSA: You are owed nothing.

NATALYA: What! You must —

PAVEL: Give it to me!

SEMYON: [*gently*] Listen, Mother, it's the law. It's our inheritance.
You can't just —

VASSA: You've lost your inheritance. [*Pause.*] The will leaves everything to me. Doesn't it, Mihail?

MIHAIL: Yes, that's quite right.

NATALYA: But — but they must have forged it!

VASSA: In sole, unrestricted ownership.

MIHAIL: [*business-like*] Witnessed by Father Yegor, Antip Stepanov
Muhoyedov, who you know, and Ryzhev, the landowner. All,
I assure you, quite above board.

SEMYON: But — but it must be a mistake! We can't be treated like
this . . . Where are the papers? Show us proof!

MIHAIL: Here, I have copies for you. [*produces copies of the will from
his pocket*] The original, of course, is in safe keeping with the
notary. Semyon, your copy. Pavel.
[*He offers PAVEL a copy.*]

PAVEL: I don't want it. I don't want to see it. I don't care any more.
I knew I'd never be free. This cursed business — nothing ever
came of it. Nothing ever will.

NATALYA: [*weeping*] Oh, Semyon, Semyon, we're ruined!

VASSA: Well, Pavel?

PAVEL: Oh, yes, you've cornered me all right. No choice, have I?
At least monks don't live in hell — like this . . .

MIHAIL: They live a very good life, I think . . . you'll be happy there.

PAVEL: Well then, Liudmila, so it really is good-bye. One more
kiss, eh? Just to show how kind you are. A last kiss.

LIUDMILA: Of course . . .

[*She goes to him.*]

PAVEL: [*suddenly rough*] A real kiss, eh? Not on the forehead. Here —

[*He grabs her.*]

LIUDMILA: No! No! Don't touch me!

PAVEL: I thought so. I still disgust you, don't I? I won't touch you. I won't see you again, any of you!

[*He rushes off.*]

VASSA: Mihail, quick, keep an eye on him, he could do anything the state he's in.

MIHAIL: Of course. Oh, and do you want me to announce Prokhor Ivanovich's death?

VASSA: Yes, of course. Peacefully. Natural causes.

MIHAIL: Of course.

[*He exits.*]

SEMYON: So — for us nothing has changed. We must continue. . . I don't know what to say —

VASSA: No, you wouldn't. Ah, go along with you. You'd be lost without your mother — and that silly wife of yours.

NATALYA: [*reluctantly bowing, rather formally, to VASSA*] Forgive me, Vassa Petrovna, if anything —

VASSA: That'll do, now get out, both of you, before I get angry with you.

[*SEMYON and NATALYA exit.*]

Oh, dear God, I'm tired, so tired . . .

[*Exhausted, she begins to sway on her feet, and looks for a moment as if she might fall. ANNA rushes over to her and helps her to sit.*]

ANNA: Mama, are you all right?

VASSA: Water — just fetch me some water. I feel a little faint.

ANNA: Here, sit down. Liuda, get some water.

LIUDMILA: Of course!

[*She exits.*]

ANNA: Honestly, Mother, you'll wear yourself out!

VASSA: No, no, I'm just tired. It's hard, Anna, so hard. He's my son. You understand that? My son.

ANNA: Yes, I know, but when you suddenly came up with the idea of the monastery. It was a miracle!

VASSA: Suddenly! Dear God, for years I've been trying to think what I could do with him, how he could be happy . . . night

after night I've lain awake, thinking, thinking. No, there are
no miracles in this world, Anna. Only those we make for ourselves. You must realise that yourself by now, after what you've
just done.

ANNA: Yes, now I do.

[*LIUDMILA returns with the water.*]

VASSA: Ah, thank you, Liudmila.

LIUDMILA: My God. There's a dead man in the house, our world
has almost fallen apart and I feel — happy! Oh, Mother, what
wonders you've done for me!

VASSA: Happy?

LIUDMILA: Yes, I feel — oh, I feel I can start life all over again!

VASSA: You shall. But you will stay with me, won't you? Put the
past behind you. Find yourself a good man, marry him. You'll
find one, I promise. And you'll have children, and they'll be
my grandchildren . . . I'm very fond of you, Liudmila. I may
have been harsh with you, but you know that. You too, Anna,
come and live here with your children. God knows, I've had
no luck with my sons. So I'll live for my grandchildren instead!
And the garden — it will be used as it should be. For children
to play in. Listen — what was that?

ANNA: What? I can't hear anything.

VASSA: I thought . . . I've been a wicked woman, I know that. I've
had to fight, and I've been ruthless too. Dear God, yes. True,
I've had cause to fight, always, I've needed to . . . even so, even
when you win, you still feel, well, sorry for what you've done.
Do you love me, eh? Either of you? Just a little? I don't ask
for much. But I am human, and my Pavel, my own son — is
that him? He's calling me, I can hear him!

LIUDMILA: No, Mother, there's no one. No one is calling.

ANNA: It's all quiet now. Just rest.

VASSA: Funny, I thought . . . No. There's no rest for me. I'll never
be able to rest. Never.

THE END